GODLY PLAY

IN MIDDLE AND LATE CHILDHOOD

CHERYL V. MINOR

FOREWORD BY
Jerome W. Berryman and **Heather Ingersoll**

CHURCH
PUBLISHING
INCORPORATED

Church Publishing
19 East 34th Street
New York, NY 10016

Cover design by Jennifer Kopec, 2Pug Design
Typeset by PerfecType, Nashville, Tennessee

Library of Congress Cataloging-in-Publication Data
Names: Minor, Cheryl V., author. | Berryman, Jerome, writer of foreword.
Title: Godly play in middle and late childhood / Cheryl V. Minor ; foreword
   by Jerome W. Berryman and Heather Ingersoll.
Description: New York, NY : Church Publishing, [2022] | Includes
   bibliographical references.
Identifiers: LCCN 2022003079 (print) | LCCN 2022003080 (ebook) | ISBN
   9781640655799 (paperback) | ISBN 9781640655805 (epub)
Subjects: LCSH: Christian education--Philosophy. | Play--Religious
   aspects--Christianity. | Christian education of children.
Classification: LCC BV1464 .M55 2002 (print) | LCC BV1464 (ebook) | DDC
   268.01--dc23/eng/20220304
LC record available at https://lccn.loc.gov/2022003079
LC ebook record available at https://lccn.loc.gov/2022003080

Contents

Foreword

An Introduction to Cheryl Minor

I first met Cheryl Minor at a Godly Play workshop in 1992 at Christ Church Cathedral in Houston, where I served as canon educator. Only a few years later, Cheryl and her husband, Paul, became the co-rectors of All Saints in Belmont, Massachusetts, in 1997, and in 2000, Cheryl became a Godly Play Trainer.

There are three reasons Cheryl is the most qualified person to write this book. First, she has been working with Godly Play in the parish context since ordination.

All Saints also hosts the Global Montessori School, where Cheryl teaches Godly Play, for families who elect this experience, and music. Cheryl holds a BM in Music Education from Boston University and was a voice major. This involvement in the Montessori school keeps the halls of the church ringing with the sounds of children during the week and keeps Cheryl in touch with the Montessori roots of Godly Play.

The second reason Cheryl is the one to write this book is her broad and deep experience with Godly Play. Since becoming a Trainer in 2000, she has helped lead nearly every phase of Godly Play's mission to help guide children's play with God, from being the liaison with Godly Play Resources, where the Godly Play materials are made, to leading the Education Committee, and now leading the Center for the Theology of Childhood.

Most importantly, Cheryl is leading the revision of the volumes of *The Complete Guide to Godly Play*. This means that she is profoundly aware of both individual lessons and the whole sweep of the spiral curriculum. She is working with the Rev. Dr. Rosemary Beales, who recently spent twelve years as lower school chaplain at St. Stephen's and St. Agnes School in Alexandria, Virginia. The three of us are almost finished with this daunting task.

The third reason Cheryl is fully prepared to write this book is because of the training she received working on her Ph.D. Her thesis was entitled, "Promoting Spiritual Well-Being: A Quasi-Experimental Test of Hay and Nye's Theory of

Children's Spirituality." This was one of the first empirical tests of the claims of Hay and Nye's classic theory that relate to the nurture of children's spiritual well-being. (Dr. Rebecca Nye is a child psychologist and Godly Play Trainer in the UK.)

Cheryl's study tested two claims: that exposure to six conditions posited as fostering relational consciousness in a program of spiritual formation (Godly Play) promotes spiritual well-being and that the effect continues after exposure ends. The results were encouraging and lend support to the theory that Godly Play promotes spiritual well-being in children both during their time in the program, and after they leave it.

—Jerome W. Berryman, founder of Godly Play

An Introduction to This Book

When I began my work in children's Christian formation almost twenty years ago, I had an insatiable desire for resources to help me deepen my practice. I was dissatisfied with the practical books on children's ministry, which never touched on the heart of what I was experiencing in my work with the children. Every Sunday, I sat with children open and ready to make meaning, ask hard questions, wonder about their worlds and God, and create and contribute. Whether it was from a theological, pedagogical, or developmental framework, the resources never went deep enough to speak to the depth and complexity I regularly experienced with the children.

Eventually, I found a home in the literature on children's spirituality. As the field of childhood studies burgeoned in the 1960s, a new approach to researching childhood spirituality soon emerged. The seminal work of Robert Coles, David Hay, Rebecca Nye, and Brendan Hyde offered qualitative analyses of the complex spiritual lives of children. Yet, even twenty years later, the resources available to support the practices of children's Christian formation largely remained stuck in a framework focused on content acquisition, entertainment, or a simplified and limited view of developmental stage theories missing the growing discourse on the spiritual capacity of children.

Godly Play offered a unique resource, bridging the gap between theory, research, and practice. In 1991, *Godly Play: A Way of Religious Education* by Jerome

Berryman was first published. The book is about "religious growth and how to foster it." It goes on to share, in great detail, a method developed by Berryman, inspired by Maria Montessori and Sophia Cavalletti. In an unprecedented way, this publication weaved together theology, pedagogy, and research as the undergirding of a very defined approach to religious formation with children, which Berryman had tested and honed in circles of children for many years.

Thirty years after that publication, Godly Play grew to a global network of religious leaders, educators, chaplains, and parents committed to being with children and providing a space for children to explore their spiritual experiences and existential questions. Berryman has since published a number of both academic and practical books. These books continue to build on Berryman's original *Godly Play* volume, drawing upon more research and theory to support and enhance the practice of Godly Play and offer new insights for a discourse on the theology of childhood.

As we look back on the use and growth of Godly Play over the last thirty years, the Godly Play Foundation is in the process of exploring new insights we have gained over the years. Dr. Cheryl Minor, a Godly Play Trainer, storyteller, and director of the Center for the Theology of Childhood, grew increasingly concerned by the observation that many organizations value and use Godly Play for young children but often abandon it for children in middle and late childhood. Yet, middle and late childhood is perhaps one of the most crucial developmental stages for children to experience a space that allows them to explore their existential questions of meaning, loneliness, death, and identity. Cheryl set out to write this book, pointing to the unique challenges of Godly Play with older children while showing the reader "why it is worth it."

There is no one more equipped to author this text. Cheryl Minor's extensive experience as an Episcopal priest, educator, researcher, academic, and most importantly, Godly Play storyteller allows her to embrace this topic with a unique depth of experience and thought. After years of following her work, I now have the privilege of working with Cheryl at the Godly Play Foundation. Her unwavering commitment to centering, honoring, and trusting the child is evident in all her work and is the cornerstone of this text.

Cheryl's understanding of the unique experiences of children in middle and late childhood is grounded in her ability to listen and learn from them after many years of sitting regularly in circles with them. Cheryl frames the insight she gains from the children in her comprehensive study of psychology, attachment theory, Montessori, and the Godly Play literature. She peels back the multiple layers of societal, familial, and interpersonal pressures that undergird much of children's experiences in this stage of life to get to the heart of who they are and why they engage in ways often foreign to those of us well past those years.

Based on this wisdom, Cheryl builds on the practical guide to the method of Godly Play as articulated in Berryman's *Teaching Godly Play* by going through each component of a Godly Play session. She offers specific examples and ideas, inviting Godly Play mentors to reframe their perceptions and curate environments that allow children to enter the spiral curriculum, including the story, the wondering, the response, and the feast in meaningful ways. These examples are born out of tools Cheryl and others have used to mitigate challenges in their Godly Play sessions. Finally, this book culminates with my favorite chapter. Cheryl gives evidence for why this is so important by sharing unique insights into the long-lasting impact of Godly Play through quotes from interviews with young adults who participated in Godly Play circles as children. Building on the foundational literature of Godly Play, this book is a much-needed addition to continuing the practice of Godly Play. It is just the book I longed to read twenty years ago when I was first starting my work with children.

—Heather Ingersoll, Executive Director, Godly Play Foundation

Acknowledgments

I must begin by thanking the people of All Saints' Church in Belmont, Massachusetts, who have always supported the work of Godly Play, not just at All Saints', but all around the world. A special thank you goes out to the children of All Saints' (including my own daughter and son!) who have blessed me for years by joining me in the circle to wonder about the stories of God. The lessons I learned from them fill the pages of this book.

Thank you to all those in the global Godly Play community who completed the surveys regarding your work with children in middle and late childhood. I am especially thankful for those who put us in touch with young adults who "graduated" from your programs who shared their memories and insights about how Godly Play continues to impact their spiritual lives. I am hugely indebted to my research intern, Hannah Sutton-Adams, who analyzed the surveys, conducted interviews with all the young adults, helped create the annotated list of suggested print materials, and more.

Thank you to the staff at the Godly Play Foundation who supported me throughout the writing of this book. Your words of encouragement sustained me in more ways than you know! Thanks also to my fellow Godly Play Trainers for the inspiring stories of their work with children of all ages, especially my friend Nancy St. John.

To my husband: The encouragement and space you gave me to do this work was essential to my making this book come to life. I am filled with love and gratitude for you. I am beyond blessed to be able to do life and ministry with you!

Finally, thank you to Jerome Berryman, who has generously invited me to be a part of his life-changing work for over twenty years. My work with Godly Play has been the most meaningful part of my ministry. I am forever grateful for this gift and for you.

CHAPTER 1

The Children

The goal of Godly Play is to play the ultimate game for itself. The players are God, the self, others, and nature. The place for play is at the edge of knowing and being. The time has a very clear limit. It is for our lifetime.[1]

Godly Play is a comprehensive approach to Christian formation that consists of eight volumes of lessons. Together the lessons form a spiral curriculum that enables children to move into adolescence with an inner working knowledge of the classical Christian language system intended to sustain them all their lives. Much has been said about how Godly Play is for children ages three to ninety-nine, meaning it is an approach that nurtures children and adults equally. Still, many users abandon the approach as children move out of early childhood (aged three to six). Why? Some of it is a lack of training and understanding. The name, Godly Play, is enough to make people think this must be something for young children. However, it is also because as children move into middle and late childhood (aged six to thirteen) adult mentors begin to feel some resistance from the children and their parents.

This book is about both the challenges and deep joy of doing Godly Play with children in middle and late childhood. As children move into this developmental stage, they find themselves at a significant and serious crossroads. I have strong memories of that time in life growing up as the middle child, the second of three sisters. I would often find myself looking ahead at the excitement of what growing up meant as I watched my older sister's life expand before my eyes, longing to be included in what seemed like such an exciting life. At the same time, I looked back at my early childhood through the lens of my little sister, sometimes with great nostalgia. I remember sneaking down to the playroom to play with my little sister for hours, hoping my older sister would not find us for fear of her making

---

1. J. W. Berryman, *Godly Play: An Imaginative Approach to Religious Education* (Minneapolis, MN: Augsburg Press, 1991), 8.

fun of me. Our favorite game was to create big houses with our blocks and then fill them with little wooden people, acting out their lives in great detail. I did not know it of course, but I was making meaning about all of the things that were happening in real life as we created those worlds. I knew that I was supposed to be leaving those childhood things behind, but I also knew that on some level, I still very much needed that time of uninterrupted and glorious play.

Early childhood and adolescence often get more attention than middle childhood. That is why I love a poem by Billy Collins called, "On Turning Ten." I challenge you to read it and not feel the pathos of it. Collins's poem tries to capture that feeling I had as a child, standing between my older and younger sister. He gives voice to the real grief children can feel at this stage in life as they mourn what was a seemingly simpler time. In the poem the child, who is turning ten, stands at the window, realizing that his bike that he sees leaning against the garage has lost its magic, and that even the way the light hits the landscape looks more serious. As children move into middle and then late childhood, life shifts in dramatic and complex ways for them. It is a time filled with existential anxiety and questions, as the child struggles to discover their particular meaning and purpose in life. This book is about these children, and it is a call to persevere with Godly Play, despite the resistance you may feel, because it is exactly what they need.

So, what are children in middle and late childhood like, and why do they create challenges for Godly Play mentors?

"Savvy School-Goers"

As children move out of early childhood, they spend most of their days at school. Very quickly they become what I call "savvy school-goers." It starts as early as kindergarten. If you peek into a typical kindergarten class in most Western contexts, here's what you might see: a teacher reviewing sight words with students; children reading to one another in pairs; students practicing addition or subtraction; children learning about earth or plant science; students writing in journals; children and teachers engaged in state-mandated assessments. Even art and music classes are focused heavily on teaching specific content, concepts, or skills. I am not here to argue about what is happening in the schools, because I know from talking with teachers and parents that they are all under enormous pressure to perform at a higher level academically. Everyone—children, teachers, administrators, whole school districts—is being assessed and held up to public scrutiny. What this does mean, however, is that from an early age children are learning how to succeed in that sort of environment. Success means getting the right answer in school and will for the rest of their lives. Even in schools that value creativity and independence, there are clearly right and wrong answers, and children learn early on that the right answers bring rewards. The rewards include praise from their teachers and parents, admiration from their peers, sometimes physical prizes, and for themselves a sense of accomplishment. What effect does this have on Godly Play?

Those experienced with Godly Play know that one of the distinctive features of the approach is the "wondering" done by the community of children and mentors about the lessons. We often refer to the wondering as "wondering questions," but they are not questions in the proper sense, nor are they statements. They deserve their own kind of punctuation, but there is none, so we are stuck with the question mark. The question mark is used to evoke an openness to the wondering, not to elicit a particular answer. We hope it communicates to the children that we are curious about what they are thinking about the lesson and that the Godly Play Room is a safe place to share those thoughts. That safe place is created by valuing every answer that is offered, as opposed to choosing the right answer. Once children start going to school, however, they often struggle to trust that. School convinces them that there must be a right answer, and if they are not sure what that is they will often just say nothing. Furthermore, they begin to be very aware of their peers and worry that if they say something wrong, they will look silly in front of them. This can also cause them to say what they *know* are silly or outrageous answers in order to make their peers laugh.

When volunteer mentors begin to encounter this sort of resistance to the process from the children, they start questioning the effectiveness of the method. When presented with this information, church leaders are also quick to decide a change of curriculum is needed. I will talk more about what the mentors can do when this begins to happen in chapter 4 on leading the session, but for now it is simply enough to name the challenge.

"Savvy school-goers" will also struggle with the Response time during a Godly Play session. In my description of kindergarten, above, you did not see much time for open play. Children as young as five are often given just twenty to thirty minutes on the playground, and even less if you count the time it takes to move them from the classroom to the outdoor space. Furthermore, virtually every moment of their time indoors is programmed. This is compounded by the myriad of after-school programs parents feel compelled to provide for their children to be sure they are getting all they need to be successful adults (sports, music lessons, dance lessons, tutoring, and so on). They get home late, and even young children have home-work, reading, dinner, chores, and more. Then the whole family collapses in bed just to be ready to do it all again the next day.

This makes open Response time (I can do anything?) a kind of crisis for the child, especially as they move into middle and late childhood. They feel pressure to make a choice that is right, or at the least will not look silly to their peers. Suddenly the idea of coloring or painting a picture becomes very risky. Open-ended response time is already a challenge for many volunteer Godly Play mentors. They won-der how allowing the children to work with the materials freely is helping them learn anything, so when they encounter resistance to even making a choice, they quickly question the effectiveness of the method. It is often hard to really see how a child's work is connected to the lesson or to their relationship with God. Such thinking is hard to put into words, much less create a visual representation of what is going on deep inside. Trained mentors know this and learn to trust that whatever is being created is being done in the context of the room where the child is surrounded by the Christian language system, so much more is going on than meets the eye.

The Fast Pace of Life

A second challenge to doing Godly Play with children in middle to late child-hood is the ever-increasing pace of life. Not only are children and families navigating a jam-packed schedule of activities, but even the in-between time is filled with some sort of stimulation. Children as young as eight or nine are often given a smartphone, presumably for safety's sake—a way to contact a par-ent for a ride, for example—but nonetheless it means they are never without a means of entertainment. Younger children are handed tablets and phones to keep them busy while parents need to complete a task, or while waiting for an appointment or class to start. Many cars are outfitted with equipment to show movies, so just driving to the store becomes another opportunity to stare at a screen. Technology also means things are available to children almost as soon as they can think of them. I want to hear a song, I need an answer to a question, I just want to know how to spell something—all are questions or needs that can be answered in just a few moments on a smartphone or tablet. The bottom line is children are generally overstimulated and that stimulation robs them of the capacity for introspection.

It wasn't supposed to be this way. As a child growing up in the 1960s, I can remember people saying that one of the challenges of the future would be what to do with all our time. Technology was supposed to free up hours and hours of our time so that we could focus on what really matters: friends, family, fun. Instead, the opposite has happened. In recent years we have seen an amazing proliferation of time-saving innovations—airplanes, personal computers, smartphones, micro-waves, drive-through restaurants, Amazon, and the entire World Wide Web—yet the pace of life has been cranked to a level that would have been unimaginable three decades ago. All of this makes the kind of slow pace and silence that is part of a typical Godly Play session almost radical.

In recent years I have noticed increasing evidence of this as children enter a Godly Play Room. They often appear on a Sunday morning with glazed eyes as if some-one just yanked them out of bed (or more likely yanked whatever device they were looking at in the car out of their hands and sent them to Sunday school). The mentor in that situation has a herculean task to get the circle ready to hear a lesson, much less think deeply about it. The silence inherent in many of the pre-sentations is almost painful for children accustomed to so much stimulation, and so the negative behavior begins. Exploring a story more deeply, or looking at some of the print resources, are choices that do not make sense to these over-stimulated children, so work time becomes just "busy-time." The children can be seen work-ing aimlessly with the supplies that are available while chatting with their peers. In truth, they struggle to focus on anything in the room whether it is a lesson, the mentor presenting the lesson, or even their peers. The average volunteer does not have the resources to work through all of that, and so, once again, the method gets blamed.

Technology-Heavy Schools

Technology is also everywhere in education. In many school districts the traditional black board has been replaced with a "smart board," which is just a large, touch-controlled version of the teacher's computer. The teacher can pre-load notes, images, videos, and perform internet searches in real time with the children. This, naturally, speeds up everything, making downtime almost nonexistent. At the same time students are often given laptops or tablets to use in and out of school to complete assignments. The pandemic that hit in 2020 moved all learning to screens for months and will likely change the nature of education forever. By necessity, teachers learned many ways to deliver instruction via screens and my guess is a great deal of this will continue whether there is a pandemic or not.

Once again, this makes what happens in a typical Godly Play Room feel strange and foreign to children coming from a culture that has such a high value for technology and certainty. One guesses children, especially when they are new to Godly Play, come in looking for the computer center or TV. These children are baffled when asked to sit on the floor and watch a teacher tell a story with handmade materials. This gets worse when the teacher starts asking "wondering questions." Who wonders about anything these days when knowledge and information can be accessed with just a click of a button for everybody at any time?

Children whose learning during the week is so screen dependent also find open-ended work time strange. They are so unaccustomed to having the space to explore an art medium for themselves, for example, with no particular goal or product in mind that they become almost paralyzed by the choices. The idea of working with a story material is equally bizarre. They may be asked to read books in school but sitting and working with a three-dimensional version of a story could feel like something only little children do, for example the way they observe younger siblings, cousins, or neighbors building with blocks or playing with dolls. It just isn't sophisticated enough for a child who does their homework on a computer! Even those who might feel drawn to the art materials or stories will often stifle that impulse, as I mentioned earlier, for fear of looking silly in front of their peers. Instead of finding a way over this obstacle, most volunteers simply blame the method and beg for something new.

Normal Self-Differentiation

As children enter middle and then late childhood, they are deep into the process of self-differentiation: a time when they begin not simply to spend more time apart from their parents, but also begin to define themselves quite apart from their parents. This is generally referred to as normal self-differentiation, and it is a critical part of development. A helpful definition comes from Bowen Family Therapy:

> Differentiation is the process of freeing yourself from your family's processes to define yourself. This means being able to have different opinions and values than your family members but being able to stay emotionally connected to them. It means being able to calmly reflect on a conflicted interaction afterward, realizing your own role in it, and then choosing a different response for the future.[2]

Positive and healthy self-differentiation is happening when you hear people speaking their minds with thoughtful conviction even though others might disapprove. You know it is a struggle when you observe someone spending most of her time fighting against the views and values of her parents and clinging to their opposite view at all costs. It's missing when someone represses his feelings and ideas in fear of being rejected or shamed by them.

How does this become a challenge for children in Godly Play? In my experience, as children enter middle and late childhood Sunday morning becomes one of the many places where children and parents battle. The busy lives described earlier mean that children are weary of schedules and are yearning for some unscheduled time. Because of the increasing prevalence of activities scheduled on Sunday mornings (sports, birthday parties, family outings, and more), church attendance is fast becoming something that happens "when we have time." Children are quick to pick up on this, learning that church is in many ways an optional activity for their parents. This means Sunday morning suddenly feels like a place where a child can flex her newly developing skills of self-differentiation. A parent who begins to experience pushback from a child will often "dig in their heels" and expect

---

2. Bowen Family Therapy, http://www.psychpage.com/learning/library/counseling/bowen .html

compliance from the child, but that often means the child enters the Godly Play Room with a kind of "chip on their shoulder." You can see it on their faces—a defensiveness against finding anything meaningful in the process. They may not say it directly, but you can read it in their behavior. It is as if they walk in with a sign, warning the well-meaning Godly Play mentor, "I don't intend to enjoy this. I will not find anything meaningful here. I am just here because my parents said I had to come." As the battle at home continues, they may in fact start winning from time to time, especially if other parts of life are becoming a battle (for example, homework, practicing an instrument), or if one of the parents is not active in church. An astute child may suggest to the active parent, "Why do I have to go if Dad (or Mom) is staying home?" This means when they do come, they have missed important lessons, and are even more defended against the process.

As these battles rage at home, the parent, at least in my experience, is often quick to blame Godly Play. They assume that the child does not want to go because they are bored with Godly Play. The crisis hits hard when that parent calls the leadership of the parish to complain. All churches, particularly those in the mainline tradition, are struggling with attendance and giving. This leads to an attitude of "the customer is always right," and so everyone blames Godly Play, and there is a scramble to find something that will miraculously fix the situation. There may even be some small wins if the program chosen has a high entertainment value, but in the end the issues do not change, and the normal process of self-differentiation continues, leading to the same sorts of battles despite the shift in program.

The process of self-differentiation also involves "carving a place" for themselves among their peers.[3] This means they are keenly aware of how they look to their peers, what some might call "the cool factor." This can make them alternatively very shy and quiet, for fear of saying something that might make them seem too young or silly, or cause them to play the part of the clown in the circle, looking to get the approval of their peers for being especially clever. It is hard not to see how this could cause issues in a Godly Play room.

---

3. S. M. Gavazzi, S. A. Anderson, R. M. Sabatelli, "Family Differentiation, Peer Differentiation, and Adolescent Adjustment in a Clinical Sample," *Journal of Adolescent Research* 8, no. 2 (1993): 205–225. doi:10.1177/074355489382005,

Additional Factors That Inhibit Spiritual Growth for Children in Middle and Late Childhood

Godly Play with children in middle and late childhood can also be difficult because of the cultural pressures they encounter in their daily lives that devalue spirituality and religion. Research conducted by David Hay and Rebecca Nye in England on children's spirituality, for example, revealed some of the pressures that children as young as ten years old begin to feel from their peers and even well-meaning adults.[4] The children in Hay and Nye's study often spoke about the "consequences" of their spiritual experiences. Several described feeling calm, peaceful, holy, a sense of oneness, and feeling free, during and after having a spiritual experience or insight.[5] However, negative consequences were also mentioned, particularly by the older children. "Children spoke of the danger of feeling embarrassed, ridiculed or undermined as a result of exposing their experience in the public domain."[6] These were mostly predictions on the part of the children, since many told the interviewer that they rarely, if ever, spoke about these experiences with other people. Hay and Nye proposed that this is evidence of the cultural taboo regarding the sharing of spiritual experiences, which can lead children to repress and even discard spirituality altogether. They said:

> Whilst most people know they have a spiritual life, they are usually embarrassed about it, fearing they will be thought stupid, foolish or even mentally unbalanced if they speak about it in public. Our research has shown that a similar shyness is already evident in most children by the age of ten, including those who are religiously practicing.[7]

Support for this claim is provided by Brendan Hyde's study of the spiritual lives of Australian children.[8] Hyde observed factors that he suggested were inhibiting children's expression of their spirituality. For example, when children were asked what mattered most to them, "the children genuinely believed that what mattered

---

4. D. Hay and R. Nye, *The Spirit of the Child*, rev. ed. (London: Jessica Kingsley Publishers, 2006).
5. Ibid.
6. Ibid., 127.
7. Ibid., 144.
8. B. Hyde, "Weaving the Threads of Meaning: A Characteristic of Children's Spirituality and Its Implications for Religious Education," *British Journal of Religious Education* 30, no. 3 (2008): 235–45. doi: 10.1080/01416200802170169.

most to them was the acquisition of money and/or material possessions."[9] Hyde proposed that this is indicative of the consumerist culture that children, at least in the West, inhabit. He also observed what he calls trivializing, described as "the avoidance of confronting issues of meaning and value in life, as well as making light of such issues."[10] The children were heard laughing about the question, or worse showed a disinterest in the question, thinking it was unimportant. Hyde suggested that this is a reflection of the culture the children inhabit, which does not value much of anything.

How does this manifest itself as a challenge in Godly Play? I have observed in recent years a growing sense in children that what we are doing in Godly Play is not valued in the world they usually inhabit (school and even at home). You can see it in all the ways children in middle and late childhood approach the process, including how they respond during the Lesson, the Wondering, Response time, and even during the Feast. In general, it manifests itself in harmless ways, such as silly comments about materials. It gets more problematic when a child, or the whole circle, laughs at one child's serious comment. A child may also simply opt-out, making a decision, for example, to try and sit outside of the circle, suggesting to the others in a nonverbal way that whatever is happening in the circle is unimportant. Children will also sometimes resist making a choice during work time, bringing with them a book to read from home for instance. All of this presents a challenge to the Godly Play mentor, who is seeking to not only engage the child in question, but also battling the effect that behavior has on the whole community of children. Even those (or perhaps especially those) who are interested in participating in the process may feel stifled in the presence of a child who is trivializing the experience, not willing to risk being laughed at. It only takes one child to stifle all the children in the circle. Finding the strength to trust the process in the face of this kind of resistance is hard for even the most seasoned Godly Play mentor, not to mention one who is new to the practice. The real issue is that no matter what the mentor does, it does not disappear altogether. Children are under enormous

---

9. Ibid.
10. Ibid., 236.

pressure from the world that devalues anything spiritual, but I do believe that our efforts make a difference even when we cannot see the evidence.

Now that we have described most of the challenges that make doing Godly Play with children in middle and late childhood difficult, we will turn our attention to the ways the Godly Play method is particularly designed to help the children navigate this time in their lives, how Godly Play mentors, church leadership, and parents can respond to the challenges, and why it is worth it.

CHAPTER 2

The Environment

The objects surrounding the child should look solid and attractive and "the house of the child" should be lovely and pleasant in all particulars. It is almost possible to say that there is a mathematical relationship between the beauty of the surrounding and the activity of the child. He will make discoveries rather more voluntarily in a gracious setting than in an ugly one.[1]

One of the hallmarks of the Godly Play method is the attention given to the environment. By environment I am referring to the physical space used for Godly Play as well as the quality of materials used for both the lessons and response to the lessons. In this chapter I will describe why the environment is especially important for children in middle and late childhood and how a Godly Play room can be designed to meet the needs of this age group.

Adult Sacred Space

In most congregations, real effort and care is taken with the space provided for adults to worship. Take a moment to reflect on the sacred space that means the most to you. What is it about that space that enables you to come close to God? It could be the way the light shines through the windows. Perhaps it is the windows themselves, if they are stained glass, communicating without words the stories of the People of God. In most places the wooden pews may be uncomfortable, but even the smell of the wood polish might evoke deep memories for you as you think of all the important moments that happened for you in that space. What else calls to you as you reflect on that space? Are there important symbols, such as a brass or wooden cross, a table, a lectern? Why do we put so much time and thought into the creation of these sacred spaces for adults? Rebecca Nye suggests that "We do these things because, indirectly, they express our theology, our

---

1. M. Montessori, *The Child in the Family* (New York: Discus/Avon, 1970).

understanding of God's nature and our desire to relate to that. We're avoiding being *careless*—and this says we think that God is worth caring about."[2]

What does it feel like when you walk inside such a place? I know that for me, my heart slows down a bit as my eyes grow accustomed to the light, and then, I feel something deep inside; I feel the prayers of all the years surrounding me, the echo of the music that often soars in this place from the great pipe organ, and the connection not just to God, but also the community that gathers in that place with me to support one another on our spiritual journey. This might sound strange, but the space feels both safe and a bit dangerous. Dangerous because of how close I can feel to God in that place, whose presence is at the same time comforting and mysterious; someone who my mind cannot quite grasp because I am human. We often refer to such spaces as sacred because of all that has been said, but also because it is a place set apart from all that is ordinary.

The Typical Sunday School Room: The Unspoken Lesson

The typical Sunday school room is anything but beautiful. In the best of circumstances, it is clean and bright, but often the rooms are in the basement, filled with used furniture, and harshly lit. The carpet (if there is one) is generally old and stained, and the resources are limited. Growing up I went to a Sunday school like that. I know I was not harmed by the experience. The volunteers recruited to teach us were some of my favorite adults in the church, and they devoted themselves to us and the lessons they taught us. But there was a strong sense that the real stuff was happening elsewhere, and we were simply in "school" until we were ready for it. The space itself was a "lesson." It was in the parish hall (we called the undercroft) and I remember helping to set up a folding table around which we gathered. It communicated the sense that what happened there was not especially important.

Unfortunately, this type of space and the allocation of resources also points to a darker truth, and that is how undervalued children are in most communities of faith. Berryman writes:

---

2. R. Nye, *Children's Spirituality: What it is and why it matters.* (London: Church House Publishing, 2009), 43.

When we walk into a room, the colors, the arrangement of the furniture, the light, the odors, the noise, the taste on the tip of the tongue, the shape of the room, and other perceptions combine to "speak" to us. We notice how the room is cared for. Is it clean and orderly? Are things torn or broken? We notice much more than we can make an inventory of, but what this all adds up to is the sum of the values that are embedded in the room. . . . Children are even more vulnerable to this communication than we adults are. At some level they notice whether the room is clean, orderly, and in good repair. This communicates to them whether the people in charge of the room really care about the place they have entered. That in turn suggests to the children whether they will be cared for there or not.[3]

No doubt there is "lip service" paid to the fact that we ought to have something for children if we want to attract new families, but that is often where it ends. Real resources are spent on adult things or buildings, and what's worse is what is happening for and with children is often invisible to the majority of the community.

The Godly Play Room: The Unspoken Lesson

In contrast to the room described above, the goal of Godly Play is to create beautiful spaces for children. The optimal room should be filled with low shelves, with the materials carefully placed. You should be able to "read" the room, meaning you can see what is most important (the focal shelf), and easily locate the Sacred Stories, the Parables, and the Liturgical Action lessons. One of the young people interviewed as part of research for this book spoke about the space saying, "There was a lot in the room, a lot of stuff. But it was organized neatly and it felt accessible."

Art supplies used for Response time should be of high quality, and placed on the shelves in a way that invites exploration and ease of use. The materials and colors are natural, as opposed to the plastic and primary colors found in a typical room for children. The colors and images that are seen connect to the worship of the church. Walking into a room like this is very much like walking into the sacred spaces prepared for worship; it is a place set apart from the ordinary things of

---

3. J. W. Berryman, *Godly Play: An Imaginative Approach to Religious Education* (Minneapolis, MN: Augsburg Press, 1991), 80.

childhood. The unspoken lesson to all who enter is that the children in this community are valued, and what happens in this place is not just practice for the years ahead but is indeed "the real thing," so to speak.

The emphasis on the preparation of this sort of environment is rooted in the Montessori method. In her book *The Secret of Childhood*, Maria Montessori describes several important components of the prepared environment.[4] Among the most important, as far as Godly Play is concerned, is beauty. Montessori environments (and Godly Play Rooms) are prepared to allow the child maximum independence, but are also prepared beautifully and simply, free of distractions, to invoke the feeling of peace and tranquility. We believe that as children encounter these stories and respond to the stories in community and then independently, they don't just learn about God, but come close to God just as we do in worship. The space needs to be prepared with this in mind.

Maria Montessori also believed that nature should be used to inspire children, and so natural materials are a feature of any Montessori environment, including a Godly Play Room. These materials include real wood, metal, bamboo, cotton, and glass, rather than synthetics or plastics. We also recommend keeping the images on the walls in the room simple, opting for real art as opposed to cartoon biblical drawings or murals. I believe this is key to communicating to children in middle and late childhood that what is happening in the Godly Play Room is serious work. These are not the religious-themed toys you might find in a church nursery, such as plastic, multi-colored Arks. Instead, we choose wooden materials to tell the stories and keep them in wicker baskets or on wooden trays. In Godly Play we are also becoming increasingly aware of the importance of examining any of the materials we place in the room for implicit bias, searching for images that reflect the diversity of humanity rather than focusing on the Euro-centric kind of religious art that is often found in a Sunday school room.

---

4. M. Montessori, *The Secret Life of Childhood* (New York: Ballantine Books, 1982).

A Godly Play Room in Belmont, Massachusetts

These beautiful materials have a great impact on the way children respond to the stories. I am reminded of the time I brought the Godly Play Ark, a beautiful piece of art as opposed to a toy, into the hospital room of a child suffering from chronic illness. We cleared a space on his bed and I laid out the big brown underlay and told him the story of the Ark and the Flood (*The Complete Guide to Godly Play, Volume 2*, Lesson 6). He helped move the figures, and when I skipped the part about the raven he said, "Wait, wasn't there a raven?" This boy knew his Bible stories! He loved the end when everything was ready for a new start, but he thought the flood was the most important part. . . or maybe when God came close to Noah.

When I was putting things back in my bag, he picked up the Ark. He loved how smooth it was and commented on its weight.

I said, "You know, I know the guy who makes those. His name is Mike. He would love to see you playing with it."

He asked about Mike, where he makes the Arks and where he lives. Then he said, "You know this Ark is such a safe boat, it's too bad Jesus didn't have it."

I said, "What would Jesus do with it?"

He said, "He could have hidden in it when they were looking for him to kill him. It would have been perfect."

I said, "It is a very safe boat."

I don't think a brightly colored, plastic Ark would have had the same response.

Mike's Ark, handmade in Ashland, Kansas (sold by Godly Play Resources)

The reality of many Godly Play Rooms, however, is often very far from the goal, and I believe this has a direct impact on the way children in middle and late childhood will engage. In my work as a Godly Play Trainer, I often get sent to lead Godly Play training in congregations whose rooms look nothing like a Godly Play Room. Parable boxes are stacked in a corner and often have missing pieces. The other materials are in a jumble on some shelves, and the art supplies are equally disorganized or unusable (dried out markers, broken crayons, faded construction paper, and so on). What is the unspoken lesson of such a space? Berryman writes,

> When we ask children to get dressed up and come to a special place on a special day, we must be careful, for we are teaching something. The question

always is, "What is the hidden curriculum? Does it match what we intend to teach? Do the spoken and the unspoken lesson teach the same values?"[5]

While perhaps the very youngest children will overlook some of this, the older children will immediately recognize, by what they observe, that what is happening in this space is just not important and begin to clamor for something else. You will know this by their misbehavior, or simply by their absence. Parents and leaders may not fully grasp why but will in a short time blame Godly Play for all of this and pivot toward a different curriculum.

It is true that some of this is dictated by the fact that spaces are shared with other groups, or resources to create the optimal space are limited. These things are not easily changed, but just making an effort with the space will make a big difference. It can be as simple as rolling out a clean carpet in a corner of the parish hall, and carefully placing the focal shelf so that the space is well-defined. Equally important is making sure the response materials, however simple, are of a high quality and are accessible.

Whatever your space may be—a dedicated room, a shared space with other programs, a corner in a drafty parish hall—a plan to maintain that space is crucial. In so many churches the programs for children are under-resourced when it comes to staff or rely solely on the time of volunteers. While the hope is that the Godly Play mentors and children will leave the space ready for the next session, the reality is that with time pressures (the rush to get ready to go into worship, or the rush to get on with the rest of the day!), this is not a perfect plan. Cleaning (dusting, vacuuming) needs to happen, and special attention must be given to the story materials and art response shelves. It is recommended that you recruit one or more people to serve as "room stewards" and that they get trained to care for the space. Some will create lists of the items that should be on each tray, or better yet, "shelf books" that have photos of how each shelf and lesson should look when it is properly put away. A photo is very helpful for someone who is not familiar with the lessons, but really wants to help care for the room. In my rooms I have photographed all the lessons just as they should look when properly placed on the shelf. Those photos are affixed to the shelf, under the tray that holds the materials for

---

5. J. W. Berryman, *Godly Play: An Imaginative Approach to Religious Education* (Minneapolis, MN: Augsburg Press, 1991), 83.

the lesson. That way, when it is time to return the lesson to the shelf, the children and Godly Play mentors (volunteers who also need help remembering where to put things) simply walk down the shelves, looking for the picture that matches the material they are holding. This is, in a sense, creating a "control of error" for the room, which is integral to any Montessori material. A "control of error" is generally built into the lesson in some way, allowing the child to check her work independently and make corrections as necessary.

Some argue against the photos, suggesting that the children should be taught how and where to put the materials back. It is true that in an ideal scenario the children would know where all the lessons belong. Jerome Berryman writes that when this is internalized, along with the lessons themselves, children "have available to them a working model of the language system to think with and to use in discussions with others about what is important in life and death."[6] For this reason it is important for the storyteller to name the lesson as he or she takes it from the shelf, and to even name the shelves, for example saying, "Here are the Parable shelves." Indeed, if children are blessed with experience of Godly Play through early, middle, and late childhood, they do begin to internalize the way the room and story genres are organized. I have seen a child who had Godly Play in a church in California, for example, walk into my rooms in Massachusetts with great joy saying, "Oh look, everything is here!" Several of the young people interviewed for this book, when asked about their favorite story, said, "I just can't remember, but if I could walk in the room I would know immediately." It reminds me of my own experience as a young adult visiting the little Episcopal church in the town where my college was located. Like the child who found everything as it should be in the Godly Play Room, I was so comforted to find the Book of Common Prayer in this place far from home, and hear the words I had come to love as a child in that place. The goal is for the children to know where things "live" in the room, but as with most Montessori materials, creating this type of "control of error" in the room with the photographs simply makes the children more independent from day one. It is especially crucial to build in some of these tools in today's church environment, where attendance on Sundays is spotty, making it difficult for a child to remember where

---

6. J. W. Berryman, *Teaching Godly Play: How to Mentor the Spiritual Development of Children*, rev. ed., ed. C. Minor (New York: Church Publishing, Inc., 2009).

things go from week to week. Think, for example, of a child who comes just once a month, or only when spending the weekend with Mom. This child will often miss certain stories and need some assistance to navigate the space with independence.

Finally, it is a good practice to do an annual inventory of the lessons in preparation for the start of the program year, and to do it early in the summer. That way you can place an order for replacement parts if need be, and have everything ready for the start of Godly Play at the beginning of the program year.

The question for this book is not just how to build a better environment, but also how that environment can better serve children moving through middle and late childhood. How do we signal to children in middle and late childhood that Godly Play is not just something for little children? Let's turn our attention to some very specific ways the room can change to achieve this goal.

Godly Play Rooms for Middle and Late Childhood

The Godly Play method does not need to change dramatically as children enter middle and late childhood. The shape of the session remains the same: building the circle, hearing a lesson, wondering about the lesson, responding to the lesson individually, gathering for a feast, and going out with a blessing. We still sit on the floor in a circle to hear the story, and all the materials they used as young children are present. However, there is much we can do to signal to children without saying a word that what we are doing has shifted, that as they grow up so does Godly Play.

The first major change I recommend is getting some taller shelves, or shelves with at least three levels. Why? Because you are going to want to start adding extension and enrichment materials to the already familiar Core Lessons in the room. The top shelves will look exactly like the shelves in a room designed for younger children, but below those top shelf stories (the Core Lessons) you can begin to place stories and materials that extend those lessons. For example, in *The Complete Guide to Godly Play*, Volume 6, there are lessons about Old Testament figures such as Abraham, Sarah, King David, and the Prophet Isaiah, just to mention a few. The lessons about Abraham and Sarah (*The Complete Guide to Godly Play*, Volume 6, Lessons 2 and 3) extend the lesson we call "The Great Family" (*The Complete Guide to Godly Play*, Volume 2, Lesson 7), and so are placed under that lesson to show they are connected (see the photo below). Under the Extension Lessons you will want to add books, puzzles, artwork, and other print material that extend or enrich the stories above. You can see how very quickly the shelves will get full, thus making the need for taller shelves necessary. You will find detailed diagrams of the shelves in a room designed for children in middle and late childhood in Appendix A, p. 111, and an annotated list of recommended print material in Appendix D, p. 131. The taller shelves also communicate nonverbally that you are expecting older (and taller) children in this room!

This photo is of the Sacred Story shelves showing the Core Lessons all across the top, and the extension materials on the second and third shelves.

Many ask when the children will be ready for the extension and enrichment materials. I will discuss this at length in the next chapter on the spiral curriculum, but for now you simply need to know where these lessons are. These lessons are sprinkled throughout the eight volumes of *The Complete Guide to Godly Play*, but most can be found in Volume 6, 7 and 8. A complete listing of all the published Godly Play lessons is in Appendix B, p. 121.

Other ways to signal that this is a room where older children work is to add some cushions or low chairs to use during the story presentations. Children love grabbing a cushion to sit on or just lean on during the story. I have even had some of my older children start to complain that it hurts to sit on the floor, which sounds crazy, but often is true. Some will begin to lose some of their flexibility as they get older or may discover that sitting cross-legged is difficult in certain clothes, for example, in a shorter skirt. I have a child in my room who is a rising tennis star and has shown up on Sundays with some serious injuries that make sitting on the floor difficult. Being prepared with some alternative ways to be in the circle is important and is an opportunity to show that you take them seriously when they fuss about sitting on the floor (even if they are just testing you!).

We often have "kneeling tables" in rooms for younger children, and the same is true in a room prepared for children in middle and late childhood. A kneeling table is just what it sounds like—a table that is low enough to the ground that a kneeling child can comfortably work on its surface. Adding some low chairs for these tables is also advisable for the same reasons listed above regarding the circle. In my experience, children of all ages, but particularly children in middle and late childhood, will gravitate to the tables. This is likely due to the fact that they are used to working at tables at school, and/or because working on the floor seems babyish to them. While I don't want to fill the room with tables since it detracts from the ability to "read the room" with regard to the lessons (the inability to see the sweep of the Sacred Stories, for example, because the tables block the view, or the gleaming gold Parable boxes), I have added a few more tables in my rooms for children in middle and late childhood because it was becoming a competition to get a coveted spot at a table.

Another welcome addition is a couple of cozy reading spots in the room, equipped with some cushions or a low chair. In chapter 1 I wrote about how difficult the open response time can be for some children who become self-conscious about choosing an art response as they move into middle and late childhood. Having some other options, such as print material they can look at that enriches or extends the lessons in the room, can be a useful alternative to the art materials, and a cozy spot to retreat to in the room makes that even better!

A Room for Mixed Ages

Preparing a separate room for children in middle and late childhood is not always possible. There can be a simple lack of space, or it could be the numbers of children are so low that it is necessary to have all ages in a single room. There are some benefits to having the older children in the same room with the younger ones, as in true Montessori fashion the older ones model how to navigate the space for the younger ones. However, it does make it challenging on a number of levels.

Adding enrichment and extension materials to the room can complicate the space for the younger children. They cannot help but wonder about the lessons on the lower shelves, and even though they may not have heard them yet, will take them off the shelves unless there is some sort of boundary set. I will often say to the younger children during work time, for example, that only top shelf stories can go in the desert to avoid the "pig pile" of items that will get tossed in the sand by the younger children in their excitement. Art supplies that "call" to older children may also not always be appropriate for the younger ones. For this reason, I often have a shelf that is for the older children in a corner of the room, or perhaps right outside the room, filled with some of the more sophisticated materials that only the older children have access to.

Conducting an Audit of the Space

I invite you to consider a brief exercise to "audit" the space you are currently using for Godly Play. Start by going to the worship space in your congregation. Sit in your favorite spot and ask yourself the following questions:

- What makes a place "sacred"?
- What makes the church "sacred"?
- What does this space say to you about God?
- What is central here?
- What is most valued in this place? How do you know?

Now go to the space you are currently using for Godly Play. Sit in a corner of the room and ask yourself:

- What makes this space "sacred"?
- What words would you use to describe the feel of the room?
- What do you notice first about the room? What materials "call" to you?
- What seems most important in this place? How do you know?
- Is anything distracting you? (Shelves that need tidying? A messy bulletin board? The paint color on the walls? The art on the walls? Stains on the carpet? And so on.)
- What does this room "say" about God?
- What does the room "say" about the church's view of children? How do you know?
- How does the space support the children?
- If you were to change anything in the room, what would it be?

If possible, do this exercise with the decision-makers in your congregation. If they have no experience with Godly Play, you will need to educate them about what is there, and why it is important. Spending this extra time will help as they consider how resources get allocated. I remember one church that put such a high value on this program for their older children that the rector moved to one of the smaller offices in the building so his office (a large and beautiful space) could be converted to a Godly Play Room for the oldest children in the program. I often wonder at the impact that had on the children and the entire congregation—to know that they were so valued that the rector gave up his premium real estate in the complex for them!

Conclusion

The importance of creating sacred space for children to do the big work of Godly Play cannot be underestimated. To understand the character of such places, Jonathan Z. Smith, an American historian of religions, suggested the helpful metaphor of sacred space as a "focusing lens." A sacred place, said Smith, focuses attention on the forms, objects, and actions in it and reveals them as bearers of religious meaning.[7] I wonder how this is communicated to the people who enter the space.

---

7. J. Z. Smith, *To Take Place: Toward Theory in Ritual* (Chicago: University of Chicago Press, 1987).

While a wondering question has no single answer, I want to suggest that this correlates directly to all that has been described in this chapter, particularly when it comes to the beauty, simplicity, and ordered environment we seek to create in Godly Play Rooms. Children of all ages are sensitive to the feel of a room, and the prepared environment is therefore of critical importance to support children on their spiritual journeys. It "speaks" of the value put on the children by the community, and the value given to what happens in that space by all who enter.

CHAPTER 3

The Spiral Curriculum

The Godly Play curriculum can be thought of as spiral . . . a living spiral that moves upward and outward through early, middle, and late childhood.[1]

What Is a Spiral Curriculum?

As with all aspects of the Godly Play method, the concept of the spiral curriculum finds its roots in the Montessori method. Montessori opened her first school (or "Children's House") in 1907. Based on her years working with children with learning differences (those confined to asylums and the like) she began to develop her curriculum, which became and remains a global movement. The Montessori curriculum is organized as an upward moving spiral of integrated studies, rather than a traditional model in which the curriculum is compartmentalized into separate subjects, with given topics considered only once at a given grade level. Lessons are introduced simply and concretely in the early years and are reintroduced many times over the years at increasing amounts of complexity and abstraction. With each repetition, children build on what they know about a topic, digging deeper into the details, perceiving the connections more clearly, and finally developing a deep understanding of our multifaceted world.

The concept of learning as a spiral made its way into mainstream education in the 1960s, primarily through the research and writing of Jerome Bruner, who wrote, "We begin with the hypothesis that any subject can be taught in some intellectually honest form to any child at any stage of development."[2] The theory is that learners revisit topics, themes, or subjects several times throughout their school career, and that the complexity of the topic or theme increases with each revisit. The benefits suggested by advocates of this approach are that information is reinforced each time the student comes back to it, and that it allows the student to

---

1. J. W. Berryman, *Teaching Godly Play: How to Mentor the Spiritual Development of Children,* rev. ed., ed. C. Minor (New York: Church Publishing, Inc., 2009).
2. J. Bruner, *The Process of Education* (Cambridge, MA: Harvard University Press, 1960).[AU: page number?]

move from the simple to the complex more easily. An example that is often given comes from Chinese schools, where students revisit each of the basic sciences each year. Many suggest that this is the reason their performance in those subjects is superior to American students, who study one subject per year (for example physics in the ninth grade, biology in the tenth grade, and so on).

Bruner argued for learning through inquiry (like the kind of wondering that happens in a Godly Play session), believing that the knowledge of all subjects should begin with the child's intuitive understanding of basic ideas. The curriculum should then have the child revisit or reexamine earlier learned ideas, expanding upon them. As this continues throughout the child's development, the child reaches a deeper and deeper understanding of individual ideas and how they relate to each other.

Bruner proposed that as any learner encounters new material, he or she moves through three stages: *enactive* (action-based), *iconic* (image-based), and *symbolic* (language-based). However, unlike Piaget's stages, Bruner did not argue that these stages were age-dependent, but the same for learners at any stage of development. Consider, for example, the *enactive* stage, when knowledge is stored primarily in the form of motor responses. Many adults can perform motor tasks (sewing, knitting, operating a lawn mower) that they would find hard to explain in iconic (picture) or symbolic (word) form. Visual images are used to store knowledge in the *iconic* stage. This may explain why, when we are studying a new subject or skill, it is useful to have illustrations or diagrams alongside the verbal information, in the same way that the Godly Play materials help us to both hear and think about Sacred Stories, Parables, and so on. In the *symbolic* stage, knowledge is stored as words, mathematical symbols, or in other symbol systems.

The Godly Play Spiral Curriculum

The goal of Godly Play is "for children to enter adolescence with a working model of the Christian language system internalized."[3] What do we mean by "the Christian language system?" All languages have a kind of working model or set of

---

3. J. W. Berryman, *Teaching Godly Play: How to Mentor the Spiritual Development of Children*, rev. ed., ed. C. Minor (New York: Church Publishing, Inc., 2009), 138.

rules that allow a person to use it to communicate or reflect in meaningful ways. Think, for example, of the way the English language functions to help us express ourselves. Its components are a combination of phonemes (the smallest unit of sound), morphemes (the smallest unit of a word), lexemes (words or a set of words including things such as the singular and plural of a noun), syntax (the rules that govern a sentence), and context (how the words fit into the overall structure of the language). These things, along with grammar, are used together to create meaningful communication among individuals.

The Christian language system is related to language in general, of course, but it also has its own special lexemes (Sacred Stories, Parables, Liturgical Action and Silence) that function in particular ways and a particular context (our journey as God's people). In Godly Play we believe that children come to us with experience of God and a kind of unconscious understanding of how that relates to their relationship with other people, with the world, and with themselves. What they lack is a language to talk about it. We use the spiral curriculum of Godly Play to share with them both a language and a way to practice using that language. We begin with building blocks of the Christian language system, the Core Lessons, learning how to use Sacred Stories, Parables, Silence, and Liturgical Action to reflect internally and with one another about what they in essence already know. As they become fluent in that part of the language system, they are ready to add complexity with the Enrichment and Extension material. The final step is to combine all of it to think and communicate in ways that are more complex than many Christian adults, by using the Synthesis lessons. In this way, just as in the spiral I described above in a Montessori classroom, the children move from the simple to the complex, moving the spiral upward and outward to make room for new information, experiences, and communication skills as they move through early, middle, and late childhood.

What Gives the Spiral Energy?

Much has been written and studied about how individuals can get stuck developmentally. It could be the experience of trauma that gets a person stuck, or other sorts of crisis that make it difficult for a person to continue to grow and develop emotionally or otherwise. The same is true of spiritual growth. Perhaps the most well-known scholar to talk about this was James Fowler, who described the spiritual life as a series of stages moving upward on a continuum of spiritual expansiveness.[4] Fowler described a process that can stall if the individual does not have the support to stay open to new learning. While many no longer see faith development as a strict march through stages, I have encountered people who are stuck spiritually with what I sometimes call a "Sunday school faith." What I mean by that is that they cannot hear or think about a sacred story, parable, or anything else related to the life of faith apart from what someone taught them about it in Sunday school. The crisis comes when life happens; something happens that upends that understanding and makes them question the whole thing. An example is the way some curriculums teach the story of the Ten Commandments. Children may learn at a young age what they are and that if we keep them there will be at the very least an intrinsic if not an extrinsic reward. As an adult they may discover that keeping them is much more complicated than imagined, and that no matter how hard they try it is impossible. Furthermore, even those who do manage to keep them most of the time still experience hard things, which was not the reward they expected. The Godly Play method works against this by modeling a life-long openness to new learning and understanding to imbue the spiral of spiritual growth and development with enough energy to last a lifetime. What fuels the movement of the spiral? Jerome Berryman names a number of things, but perhaps of most importance is the creative process.

The Creative Process

What is the creative process? The easiest way to understand it is to describe it. Each one of us has a "circle of meaning." When we get up in the morning, it is generally intact. Then something will happen to break that circle. The break sets the creative process in motion. The *opening* may be hard or soft. A soft break could be that you get to work and suddenly realize you've forgotten your lunch. Now you need to work out a solution to this problem and the process of scanning takes place. Will you go back home and get it? Will you buy lunch? Then you have an *insight!* Yes! I'll go out to lunch today. But where will you go? Now the *development* of your insight begins. Should you have Mexican food? Italian?

---

4. J. W. Fowler, *Stages of Faith: The Psychology of Human Development* (New York: Harper & Row, 1981).

Will you go alone or invite friends? How will you pay? Finally, you decide! Italian it is. You'll invite your good friend from the office down the hall, and you're off. All is well and your circle of meaning is whole yet again, ready for the next break.

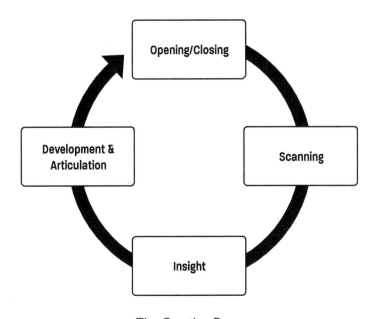

The Creative Process

The process might also be opened by the type of wondering that happens in Godly Play, and sometimes it is by something more difficult. A hard break is caused by a crisis of some sort. When this happens, Dr. Berryman writes, "We are forced to see that the meaning by which we have lived, on whatever level, has been broken."[5] A great loss, whether it is the death of a loved one, the loss of a job, or the loss of a dream, are examples of this sort of break. The work of closing the circle under these circumstances might take a lifetime. Moments of insight come, but a full and complete development and articulation of what has been understood may never come with complete clarity. I have walked with many through the process of grief, and know that while life moves forward, there

---

5. J. W. Berryman, *Godly Play: An Imaginative Approach to Religious Education* (Minneapolis, MN: Augsburg Press, 1991), 94.

are often moments when the grief comes crashing down, and the loss is felt as harshly as the day it happened. My sister, who lost her husband at a young age, will call me on those days. Often it is a milestone in the life of one of the children she shared with him that brings it all crashing down again. It is in those moments that she is struck by his absence beside her (clapping at a graduation, or sitting by them when they are sick), and she begins again the process of scanning for meaning and understanding.

All of us have certain parts of the creative process that are more comfortable than others. I know that for myself the scanning part is uncomfortable and can make me feel anxious. When I am doing the work of development and articulation I feel more in control, especially if someone else has done the work of scanning and insight for me! I know I need support (a kind of framework) and time to find the energy required of me to get into that scanning mode. Children are no different. Like all of us, they have certain parts of the circle that come more naturally to them. Part of the Godly Play mentor's role is to pay attention to that and help the children move through the entire process, so that all of it is available to them.

The Dynamics of the Godly Play Session

Just the way a Godly Play session is organized works to create a space and framework that supports the creative process. Children enter the circle and hear a story or lesson. Even when the lesson is familiar, or perhaps especially when it is familiar, the Godly Play mentor supports them by asking the wondering questions and modeling an openness to what everyone in the circle says, to see something new and think about things in a new way. All this works to set in motion the creative process in both small and large ways. Some of it will get worked out in the room, but often it just gets started there and the "working out" of the meaning happens months or years down the line.

The children then move one at a time to get out their work during response time, continuing the work of scanning for meaning, heading hopefully towards insight, then development, and finally articulation. Again, sometimes it happens in the room on that day, or another day, or sometimes many years later. The prayers and feast and then the blessing and goodbye follow. And it's ready to begin again.

How the Spiral Curriculum Works

It usually takes three encounters with a lesson for children to be able to understand it and its context in the liturgical year. Berryman writes, "Meeting a lesson three times gives children the confidence and competence to use it artfully to make meaning."[6] In the ordinary congregation, this means experiencing a particular lesson once each year, so it takes three years for a lesson to become operational in the life of a child. What happens during these three encounters?

The first year the child sees where a lesson "lives" in the room and how to get it out and put it away. This is carefully modeled by the storyteller. The second year the child remembers having seen the lesson, and signals this by saying something like, "We have seen this already. Boring." The experienced Godly Play mentor acknowledges this, saying, "It is good that you recognize it, but look how different you are from the first time you heard this. I wonder what new things you will see today. Did you know that there is always more with this kind of story?" The third year the children are so familiar with the lesson (the mechanics of it) that they can listen more closely to the words and connect them with how the teaching artifacts are moved to contribute to its ever-expanding meaning.

The first three years of seeing a story typically takes place during early childhood. During middle and late childhood, something similar happens, but,

> . . . the new learning is not so much the mechanics of the Godly Play classroom customs, but seeing the core lessons and the culture of the class from new cognitive and social developmental perspectives. In addition, the core lessons are extended during these two periods by the introduction of extension and enrichment lessons. In late childhood the third developmental period is emerging, so this new perspective makes possible the use of synthesis lessons. The Sacred Stories, the Liturgical Action and the Parables are each pulled together by one of these synthesis lessons.[7]

---

6. J. W. Berryman, *Teaching Godly Play: How to Mentor the Spiritual Development of Children,* rev. ed., ed. C. Minor (New York: Church Publishing, Inc., 2009), 121.
7. J. W. Berryman, *Teaching Godly Play: How to Mentor the Spiritual Development of Children,* rev. ed., ed. C. Minor (New York: Church Publishing, Inc., 2009), 122.

A complete listing of the lessons available to a Godly Play mentor are found in Appendix B, p. 121. There you will see all the Core, Enrichment, Extension, and Synthesis Lessons listed and where to find them.

- **Core Presentations** are *key* Sacred Story, Liturgical Action, Parable and Silence Lessons. They are placed on the top shelves in a typical Godly Play Room.
- **Extension Presentations** extend the Core Lessons or include more details. These lessons are placed on the shelf below the Core Lesson they extend. For example, the Extension Lesson about Abraham (*The Complete Guide to Godly Play*, Volume 6, Lesson 2) sits just below the Core Lesson called "The Great Family," where the children first meet Abraham and his family (*The Complete Guide to Godly Play*, Volume 2, Lesson 7).
- **Enrichment Presentations** do not extend but enrich or deepen the Core Lessons. An Enrichment Lesson goes over the same material that is in the Core Lesson from a different angle and in a more detailed way.
- **Synthesis Presentations** integrate *key* narratives to make a lesson. An example is the Sacred Story Synthesis Lesson that places four Core Lessons side-by-side to make a lesson on the Trinity (*The Complete Guide to Godly Play*, Volume 4, Lesson 19).

Knowing When It's Time to Add More Stories to Your Room

You will know the children are ready for more when they start asking for more detail. They might say to you, "But what happened after that? Or before that?" You can begin by going deeper with what you already have. This means putting stories side by side. An example of how to do that is in *The Complete Guide to Godly Play*, Volume 3, Lesson 15. Then start adding some of the Extension and Enrichment Lessons. Always take care to "hook" those stories to the Core Lesson they extend or enrich. You can do this by telling the Core Lesson one week and the Extension Lesson the next week, or you can simply stand at the shelf and remind the children about what happened in the Core Lesson and then bring the Extension Lesson to the circle to present. In general, children are ready for the Extension and Enrichment Lessons when they have worked with all the Core Lessons at least three times. This does not mean you leave the Core Lessons behind! You should still revisit those lessons from time to time, because there is always more to see and understand, especially as the children move through new developmental stages and have more and more life experiences.

Scheduling Stories

People often want help making a schedule of stories for a typical program year. Godly Play does not publish a schedule, because every program is different. Some have just one room for multiple ages, others have a more closely graded set of rooms. Furthermore, Godly Play does not try to follow the lectionary (a three-year cycle of lessons from the Bible used in many traditions). However, it can and should follow the liturgical year. If your program year begins in the fall or autumn (Late August or September in the Northern Hemisphere), you will typically use lessons from the Old Testament to begin, and then move to the Advent series. After Christmas you will tell the Parables until it is time to get ready to come close to the Mystery of Easter, the season of Lent. In other parts of the world, for example in Australia, the program year gets started in January. They often begin with the lessons for Lent and save the Old Testament lessons for their winter months. I also advise "sprinkling your schedule" with some Parables early in the year. Seeing those stories as you are working your way through the Old Testament lessons can greatly enrich the wondering and response time in the room.

This all gets a bit more complicated when you begin to add the Extension and Enrichment materials to your room(s). When Jerome Berryman first published the Extension and Enrichment materials, we asked him how to "schedule" these during the Sunday school year. He was somewhat perplexed and said, "You tell them when the children ask for them." While this might be the ideal plan, it is not practical when most of your teachers are volunteers who work hard to learn a story every week. They don't have every story in their memory bank and will need some time to prepare. Creating a schedule is going to be necessary!

If you only have one room with children of all ages, you might consider having the older children step out of the room on occasion with a storyteller to hear one of the Extension Lessons. However, if you have the luxury of creating a second space for the children in middle and/or late childhood, you can begin to schedule some of the Extension and Enrichment materials. Some program leaders are very careful planners and will plan out schedules that carry children from early childhood through late childhood, making sure all the lessons available to them get told at some point or another. I have been a bit less organized, and instead look at where we have been the year before, and plan to go someplace new in the next year. For example, if I told the Extension Lessons from the Torah (the first five books of the Old Testament) one year, then I will go back and tell the Core Lessons from that same time at the beginning of the fall and tell the Extension Lessons about the prophets the next year. Here is a sample of a story schedule just for the fall/autumn from All Saints' Church in Belmont, Massachusetts, USA, where you will see that the youngest children are told the Core Lessons only, while in the upper rooms the Extension and Enrichment Lessons are finding their way on to the schedule. The program year begins in September for this church. I have included some additional sample schedules in Appendix C, p. 125.

Sample Story Schedule

Pre-school–Kindergarten	1st–3rd Grade	4th–8th Grade
Circle of the Church Year	Circle of the Church Year	Circle of the Church Year
The Holy Bible	The Extended Holy Bible	The Extended Holy Bible
The Holy Family	The 2nd Creation	Creation
Creation	The Story of Abraham	The Ark & the Flood
The Ark & the Flood	The Story of Sarah	The Great Family
The Great Family	The Story of Jacob	The Exodus
The Good Shepherd	The Good Shepherd	The Good Shepherd
The Exodus	The Story of Joseph	The Ark & the Tent
The Ark & the Tent	The Story of Moses	The Story of Samuel
The Great Pearl	The Exile & Return	The Great Pearl
The Ark & the Temple	The Prophets	The Story of Ruth
The Exile & Return	Jonah the Backwards Prophet	The Story of David
The Prophets	The Psalms	The Psalms
Advent 1	All of Advent	All of Advent

Pre-school–Kindergarten	1st–3rd Grade	4th–8th Grade
Advent 2	The Story of St. Nicholas	The Story of St. Nicholas
Advent 3	The Story of Mary	The Story of Mary
Advent 4 + peek at Christmas	The Mystery of Christmas	The Mystery of Christmas

In the next chapter we will explore what all of this looks and feels like in real time as we consider how to lead children in middle and late childhood through a Godly Play session.

Leading the Session

In Godly Play, we enter into Parables, Silence, Sacred Stories, and Liturgical Action in order to discover the depths of God, ourselves, one another, and the world around us.[1]

In this chapter we will "walk" through a Godly Play session together, stopping along the way to describe how to support the creative process for children in middle and late childhood. In addition to my own experiences, the Center for the Theology of Childhood was able to survey several churches who have been using Godly Play with children in middle and late childhood, so we will hear from them as well. The task for the storyteller with these older, more experienced children is to keep the spiral of Godly Play moving upward and outward for the children as they move into the developmental period when language and thinking become increasingly sophisticated. This makes for interesting conversation, but also threatens their ability to stay open to the process. Some cope with the challenges these children present by moving toward a more school-like atmosphere with tables, chairs, and books. In my experience the print material is interesting for some children to work with on their own during the response time, but our time together in the circle looks remarkably like it looked when they were three and four years old.

Building the Circle

As with the younger children, it is important to start by spending the time necessary to "build the circle." This time of getting ready to shift their focus from all that swirls in their heads about family, friends, books they are reading, videos they are focused on (sometimes a video they were watching moments ago on the way to Godly Play) is even more important for these children than it is for younger ones. Life is busy and complicated for these children, which makes focusing on a story,

---

1. J. W. Berryman,. *The Complete Guide to Godly Play, Volume 2,* rev. ed., R. Beales and C. Minor, eds. (New York: Church Publishing, Inc.), 5.

and approaching it with an open heart and mind, difficult for many. As I described in chapter one, I often look at their faces as they amble into the room and see what looks like an almost glazed look in their eyes. In those moments I wonder if they were yanked out of bed to come to church, or if a parent yanked some sort of device out of their hands as they got out of the car and made their way into the church building. These children are under so much pressure with their busy schedules during the week. They are tired and need time to adjust to being in this different space.

One of the ways I try to communicate that I know they are older is by the way the room is set up. The shelves are taller, there are pillows to sit on. We gather around a beautiful, round, oriental carpet. At school, these children have long since left behind circle time on a carpet. If we can signal to them this is different by adding some things they associate with spaces for older people (oriental carpets), or a cool hang-out space in their finished basement (floor pillows), we can often overcome their initial resistance.

As the children enter the room, many will take advantage of the pillows piled up by the door and grab one to lean on. They resist making a perfect circle and just gather in clumps. I quietly remind them to make a circle, and to make room for the latecomers. A circle is important as we want everyone to approach the story from the same level and vantage point. Some struggle to sit cross-legged due to the clothes they have on (girls in short skirts, for example), or just because they are not as flexible as they once were. Depending on the children, I will sometimes allow one or two to grab a small chair.

As the circle gathers, we visit about their lives. Now is when we start paying attention not just to the physical space, but also the emotional and auditory space needed to do their work. As I begin to ask about how things are going, they often start by giving me yes or no answers, but as they become a bit more comfortable and acclimated to the space they will begin to share more about their lives. I am blessed to have been with these children for many years in this way. I know what instrument they are learning to play, their favorite subject in school, the sport they like to play, and something about their siblings and parents. There is much to talk about. This also helps to build trust among the children. As they get to know one another they become less self-conscious about sharing important insights during the "wondering" and praying together before the Feast. We are not just filling up the time with idle chitchat; we are building community.

Once I feel they are truly present, I will suggest we get ready for the lesson. As when they were small, we start by looking at the Circle of the Church Year hanging on the wall (*The Complete Guide to Godly Play*, Volume 2, Lesson 1). They are now familiar with the rhythm of the church year and like seeing the changes that are coming. One of them goes over and moves the arrow, and we look to see how far away Advent is, when it will be Easter, or how close we are getting to Pentecost. While the younger children are very focused on whose turn it is to move the arrow, the older children stop worrying about that, and are glad for the person closest to the wall-hanging to get up and move the arrow for us.

One year a child asked why other holidays were not marked on the calendar. She wanted to see when it would be Halloween and Thanksgiving, for example. I suggested she find a way to add those during work time, and she did. She got busy making a jack-o-lantern out of scraps of felt to mark Halloween, and a little turkey for Thanksgiving. She carefully placed them, looking at another calendar I had on the wall to figure out where they belonged in the Circle of the Church Year. She was so pleased with the project that she went on to mark other days like Valentine's Day, St. Patrick's Day, and the Fourth of July. We did not glue them to the calendar permanently, so at the end of her time in Godly Play I took them down. This was her work, and perhaps one day another child will get interested in doing the same, but for now it seemed important to go back to just the Sundays in the church year.

Creating a space just for the older children is, of course, not always possible, especially if you have younger children in the room with the older ones. Sometimes it is a matter of space and other times numbers. Our survey of churches using Godly Play with children in middle and late childhood indicated that a wide range of ages in a Godly Play Room is more often the case, which presents some challenges. To honor the experience of the older children, it is helpful to give them some responsibility for the session. Some of those surveyed said they would sometimes have the older children be the storytellers in the rooms. I would suggest that even your high school youth are not equipped to do that. Telling the story is just part of the process. Storytellers also need to be aware of the dynamics of the circle, they need to lead the wondering, and more. Even adults struggle to do all of that well, so asking the older youth to do it does not seem fair. Instead, I recommend finding some other ways to give them a role during the session. You could, for example, have the older ones take turns taking attendance, make them responsible for preparing the feast, ask them to sit by the youngest ones to model how to "be ready" for a story. A few of the older children in my room would take the very youngest "under their wing"—sitting with them during the story, working beside them during response time, helping them get ready for the feast, and at the end of the session walking them down to church to find their parents. Sometimes I will ask a child who was particularly engaged in Godly Play all the way through eighth grade (age thirteen in the United States) to come back as a door person when they are in high school (ages fourteen to eighteen in the United States).

One of the churches we surveyed said that they coped with the challenge of mixed ages by inviting older children to come back during the week for a session just for them, as part of a regular Wednesday offering for the whole parish. It was an opportunity to tell them some of the Extension and Enrichment Lessons, and a chance for them to wonder without the younger children present. Another of our respondents said that she felt a mixed-age group lends itself to the children naturally directing their own learning, and helping each other, which is what the Montessori method is all about. I love this story, shared by one of our respondents, about telling the Exodus story (*The Complete Guide to Godly Play*, Volume 2, Lesson 8) to a mixed-age group during Vacation Bible School in a sandbox outdoors. She writes:

> I thought they might not all sit still on the playground or might play in the sand. Instead, as we climbed into the sandbox, the older children announced that no one was going to play in the sand during the story. Everyone kept that rule and listened really well. It was hot, which I pulled into the storytelling. After wondering, I told them to run over into the shade provided by a sort of bamboo teepee. They all ran in and immediately imagined the bamboo as prison bars, shouting at the Pharoah to let the people go. That part was spontaneous and led by the older children. The next part was planned: A drum circle and learning about music as a spiritually sustaining force, as the Israelites danced beyond the Red Sea. In another bit of serendipity, we had among our children a tiny girl named Miriam. Thus, the older children

insisted she take the tambourine and lead them. I was pleased that the older kids not only participated, but also served as organic leaders in internalizing and reflecting on the story.

Even so, you will no doubt have a few children who come into the Godly Play Room very defended against the whole process, thinking that it is too babyish for them. I had one older boy come in every week with a book in his hand. Every Sunday he would try to sit outside of the circle towards the back of the room. I would gently, but firmly, tell him that was not okay. I offered to talk to his parents about having him go to the adult offering (in our case it was the first part of the Holy Eucharist). He said he didn't want to do that either. I said, "Well then choose a spot in the circle." To be fair, he was the oldest in a multi-age room, which no doubt made him feel strange. He also came from a family where church was taken very seriously, and his brother (who was three years older) was a kind of "model citizen" when it came to all of it. I'm guessing he was looking to self-differentiate from his parents and brother, carving his own path when it comes to faith. I tried to be respectful of that, while at the same time making it clear that there were some expectations even for him.

Getting the Lesson from the Shelf

After all this activity, I often ask the children to help me "make some silence" before going to get the lesson off the shelf. I usually ring a chime bell or a singing bowl, inviting the children to close their eyes. I tell them when they cannot hear the ringing anymore, they can open their eyes. I watch, and as the last child opens their eyes I say quietly, "Watch where I go to get today's story, so you will know where to find it if you want to work with it later." Other Godly Play mentors choose to sing something at this time, which can be effective with the right group. However, my experience suggests that children in middle and late childhood get a little self-conscious about singing. Another way to get ready is simply to take some deep breaths together. I do this occasionally but must warn you that it can lead to some silliness with children who are working hard to look cool, trying to convince their peers and themselves that this isn't all that important. They start competing to breathe the loudest, for example, and then everyone starts laughing. All the hard work of building the circle has to begin again! As I mentioned in chapter one, this is normal behavior for this age group. The world doesn't take things of the spirit all that seriously, so they think they should act accordingly. I find the best way to handle this is to avoid activities (like deep breathing or singing) that could make them feel silly, and to treat them with respect throughout the session. I will say more about this as we proceed through the session.

The lesson for the day begins as soon as I stand up from my spot in the circle to get the material. I remind them of the different types of stories in the room as I walk to where the material "lives." "Here are the Liturgical Lessons . . . here are the Parables . . . and here are the Sacred Stories." If the story we are going to work with comes from the Bible, I will first stop at the Transition Shelf in the room where the Holy Bible sits open to the place where the story can be found. I will say, "Here is where the story can be found in the Bible." And then after walking to the shelf where the story is I will say, "And here is where the story lives in our room."

If I plan to tell one of the Core Lessons I might say, "Today we are going to visit an old friend. Do you remember the story of . . . ? It will be interesting to find out if there is something more to see now that you are older." This honors the fact that they have seen and worked with the story before, while at the same time suggesting that a deeper engagement—a further step along the spiral—is possible. This is a way of showing respect to them; respect for their years in Godly Play and for all that they bring now that they are older. It will also, hopefully, set the stage for the creative process to begin as the children begin to scan for new insight regarding this familiar story. That is always the goal: to create an opening in their circle of meaning to make room for new insight and understanding.

In the surveys with churches using Godly Play with children in middle and late childhood, I heard that one of the biggest challenges is that the children say they are bored. Parents too will say that the children have heard all the lessons and so it's time for a new program. We all know that we are never truly "done" with a piece of scripture. One of our survey respondents told the story of a young girl who moved into the "middle room." The storyteller learned from this girl's mother that she had been talking a lot about the Mystery of Easter, wondering what it might truly be. She was very excited when the storyteller took the Faces of Easter off the shelf and began to tell it that year (*The Complete Guide to Godly Play*, Volume 4, Lessons 2–8). At the end of that series of lessons the storyteller tells the

Good Friday story, showing the children an image of Jesus wearing the crown of thorns. Then the storyteller turns the plaque over where there is an image of the Risen Christ and talks about Easter, saying that even though Jesus really died, he was with them (the disciples), and with us, "especially during the breaking of the bread." The storyteller goes on, saying, "That is the mystery of Easter. When we see the Face of Easter, we know that Good Friday is there, and when we see the Face of Good Friday, we know that Easter is there. We cannot take them apart." The little girl exclaimed, "That's it! The mystery is that you can't pull them apart!" No doubt she had seen the storyteller in the younger group do the same thing, but for the first time it made sense to her.

There is always more to see as our experiences and context change. Judy Fentress-Williams, an Old Testament scholar, speaking at the Godly Play North American Conference in 2021 spoke movingly about how the story of the Ark and the Flood (*The Complete Guide to Godly Play*, Volume 2, Lesson 6) opened up to her in new ways during the Covid-19 pandemic. Early in the pandemic she saw the Ark as a place of safety from the life-threatening virus. But during the summer of 2020, after the murder of George Floyd, she saw the Ark as a place of privilege, where only a few are truly safe.

If we are going to work with one of the Extension or Enrichment Lessons in the room, something less familiar to the children, then I take great care to remind the children of the Core Lesson or Lessons they extend. For example, if I am telling the Extension Lesson about Abraham, I will point to the Core Lesson of "The Great Family" and say, "Here is the story of the Great Family. It tells the story of Abraham and Sarah's journey in the desert and the birth of their son Isaac. Did you know there is more? Today we will learn more about Abraham, the father of the Great Family. Here is the lesson." I will then pick up the tray with Abraham's story and return to my spot in the circle.

Presenting the Lesson

The actual presentation of the lesson is not all that different from the way you would tell it to younger children. Just like the younger ones, there might be one or two in the circle that will try to take over from the storyteller. They will laugh or scoff at some part of the story, looking for a reaction from the others. Some of this is to defend themselves from the feelings that sometimes do well up from deep inside without warning. Taking all the comments and laughter seriously is the key to getting through these disruptions; acknowledging that some parts might seem strange and even funny, but then suggesting that we push that aside to see if there might be something here for all of us today. I remember telling the story of the Ark and the Flood (*The Complete Guide to Godly Play*, Volume 2, Lesson 6) to some older children, and as I raised the Ark above my head a child said, "It was a typhoon." All of the children laughed, and I simply said, "Perhaps it was like a typhoon," and moved the Ark as if the wind was blowing mightily. The laughter stopped and we were able to keep going without further interruption. Remember the goal is to push past what are developmentally appropriate defenses so that the creative process can begin.

Often the older children resist the playful wondering at the beginning of a Parable. They have "seen it before" and know, for example that the green felt in the Parable of the Good Shepherd (*The Complete Guide to Godly Play*, Volume 3, Lesson 9) is grass in the story, not a lily pad, and that the blue felt is the cool, clear, still water, not a mirror or something else. Still, I persevere. I will, however, sometimes get "above the playing" for just a moment and ask, "I wonder why we spend so much time wondering about these things?" This often makes them thoughtful for a moment and sometimes someone will say, "It helps us get ready, I guess." I nod and will say, "Yes. It certainly helps me get ready." And then we proceed.

In my experience, if I continue to deepen my focus, the children, whether young or old, follow suit. The silliness and interruptions die down, and we all enter the story together. Because these children are more experienced with Godly Play, they may blurt out a spontaneous wondering question during the story. While I might ignore that and continue on when the circle is full of little ones, I will stop and take the question seriously with the older ones. It is often as simple as looking for more detail about something. For a few years I had a couple of children in my circle who knew a lot of Bible stories. They were homeschooled and it was part of their daily routine to read from the Bible with their mother. They loved to tell me when I was leaving something important out. I would simply say, "Well there is always more isn't there?" Sometimes, however, it is more serious, like wondering why God would allow something bad to happen. Once when I was presenting the lesson on the Circle of the Church Year (*The Complete Guide to Godly Play*,

Volume 2, Lesson 2), an older child stopped me when I spoke of Jesus's death on the cross saying, "That was scary." I sat quietly for a moment to see if she would say more about it. She was quiet. I nodded to let her know I heard her, then I continued telling the story. If the conversation gets long, I'll say something like, "Let's talk more about this during the wondering. Let's finish the story now," and then focus my attention on the materials and continue.

One of those surveyed shared that she often allows the older children to choose the story they will hear. There was one year when the children asked to hear the Parable of the Great Pearl (*The Complete Guide to Godly Play*, Volume 3, Lesson 11) over and over again. She decided to surprise them by bringing in some new pearls for the story. She writes:

> I was so pleased with myself because these pearls did not have holes. I knew they would notice. When I brought out the small golden box with the new pearls one of the teenage boys said, "I am really sorry, but do you know that those are not real pearls? They are plastic." "Hmmm . . . I wonder . . . ," I said. Another boy leaned forward and picked up one of the pearls and had a good look at it. He said, "Nope, it really is plastic . . . these are not pearls." I said, "I wonder if we should hear the story anyway?" They hummed and hawed, but eventually said yes, but that I had to remember that the pearls were not real. The wondering was all about the fake pearls. When I got back home, I bought a bag of oysters, with pearls, from eBay. When they arrived, I told the story again, but this time we opened the oyster shells instead of the gold box. I doubt if the little ones would have noticed that the pearls were plastic . . . but the teenagers absolutely felt sorry that I had been scammed in my original pearl buying! We had to do the oysters with pearls again. Those pearls are very special and sometimes the older children need to take the greatest pearl home with them. It makes them smile . . . and me, too!

In *Godly Play: An Imaginative Approach to Religious Education*, Dr. Berryman writes:

> It is as if the children of late childhood want to play at three levels. There is the lesson. The lesson is important, and even if the children do not appear to focus as deeply as the little ones, there is still a lot of concentration. Second, there is the game going on about whether they will attend to the lesson. They

can play this game while still being in the lesson. The third level is the game where both you and the children know about the other two levels, so from time to time you and the children comment on that to let one another know all three games are in process.[2]

This means that with older children there is much more talking and playful banter back and forth throughout the lesson. It is a dance between acknowledging the games, while at the same time taking the story and all that surrounds it very seriously. This can be mostly accomplished by saying quite simply, "Okay . . . now are you ready?" Look around with some seriousness and then shift your focus to the story. This signals that you trust them to have fun with this and with each other, but to also find something new and important to think and wonder about together. Berryman calls this movement into the creative process (an openness to new insight and understanding) the middle-realm or the center-point. In Berryman's book *The Spiritual Guidance of Children: Montessori, Godly Play and the Future*, he writes:

> This is a place where there is "the hidden laughter of children in the foliage (TS Eliot)." It is where the creative process dwells, full of enormous potential, as the Image of God, and it is where classical Christian language needs to be absorbed and activated so it can do what it was created to do.[3]

Wondering

Wondering with children in middle and late childhood is similar in many ways to leading the time of wonder with younger children. The goal is always to stimulate the creative process and to bring to consciousness an awareness of our existential limits as human beings. The mentor models an attitude of wonder, touching the different parts of the lesson gently as the children talk about them, affirming each answer, but indicating there is always more. I often think of it as a kind of dance. As I ask a question and a child offers an answer, I move toward that child to affirm the answer, but then I move back (almost physically sitting back) to indicate there is possibly another answer, looking at the other children with expectation.

---

2. J. W. Berryman, *Godly Play: An Imaginative Approach to Religious Education* (Minneapolis, MN: Augsburg Press, 1991), 41.
3. J. W. Berryman, *The Spiritual Guidance of Children: Montessori, Godly Play and the Future* (New York: Church Publishing Inc., 2013), 87.

Berryman suggests that "When the teacher truly is wondering, the children sense wonder in the air."[4]

Many of those surveyed about using Godly Play with older children commented about how much richer the wondering time was with the older children. One of those surveyed said that it was challenging at times, because some very disturbing or provocative topics might get raised during the wondering. Sometimes, she said, she would look around at the wide eyes in the circle and realize it was time to move on from whatever they were talking about. She would acknowledge that whatever they were wondering about was hard to think about, even frightening, and then ask a new wondering question.

There are, of course, challenges involved in leading this time with older children. As I mentioned in chapter one, it is now that they begin to worry about looking silly or wrong in front of their peers. This is a real worry, because they have seen it happen to others, or experienced it themselves at school. When that happens, I put on my teacher-face and say with some seriousness, "That isn't fair. John/ Mary is being serious. This is important." I want to make it very clear that in this circle we do not laugh at one another. I often have one or two who will "take the bull by the horns" so to speak and immediately start saying the silliest thing they can think of in an effort to derail the whole thing. This is normal behavior (not children being bad). It is a reflection of the culture we all inhabit, which does not value much of anything. The best way to handle this, in my experience, is to laugh with the circle and then say, "This is fun . . . but it will also be fun to think a bit more seriously about this. So . . . I wonder what you really think?" All of this can be compounded if they don't know each other very well. That is why the time of building the circle and the feast is so crucial for this age group. The more they get to know each other on a personal level, the more open and serious the wondering will be.

Another challenge for the savvy school-goer is to believe that there is no right answer. They will sometimes get frustrated, especially when they are new to Godly Play, as the wondering continues. I remember I had a child once put his hands on his head as if it were going to burst and yell, "Isn't there a right answer!" We were all startled and sat in stunned silence for a moment. This allowed me to gather my

---

4. Ibid., 62.

thoughts. I asked, "Well . . . I wonder if we will ever know the right answer?" He sighed loudly and rolled his eyes at me. Another child said, "I think we will know when we die, because we can ask God." I said, "Hmmm . . . I wonder what your first question will be?" What followed was a rich conversation about such things as the problem of suffering, war, and all manner of evil.

During the wondering the children will oftentimes start asking questions as well. They may want to know more about the story, or the place where the story took place. One of the Godly Play storytellers at my church had a whole circle of children ask what happened to Daniel after he had all his crazy dreams. She suggested they could read the rest of the story in the Book of Daniel in the Bible. Every child chose to do that for their work. It was quite a sight to see the whole room deeply engrossed in reading the Bible during work time!

Sometimes I'll suggest they look something up in the Bible dictionary in our room or look at the maps. This helps them become confident in their own ability to find answers to the questions they have. I had a child in my circle who was very interested in maps, often spending his work time drawing maps of places he had been. When I told the story of Saul's conversion, he was struck by the part about Saul going to a "a street called straight." He asked, "Why was it called Straight Street?" I didn't know and suggested that during work time we could look on the maps in our room to see if it was a straight street. He loved that idea. It turned out that none of our Bible atlases had a good map of Damascus, so we ended up looking at google maps on my phone, and discovered that the street was indeed straight, and all the streets around it were curvy!

Another time a child recognized the words of a hymn we sang in church as I told the story of the Good Shepherd and World Communion (*The Complete Guide to Godly Play*, Volume 4, Lesson 12). I told them the hymn was actually based on one of the psalms in the Bible—Psalm 23. We decided to read the psalm. Everyone got a Bible from the Bible shelf and looked it up. They each read a verse as I moved the material accordingly. One child decided the sheepfold (the fence pictured below) needed to be around the people having Holy Communion. A second child wanted to see the two images (the psalm and the Holy Communion) side by side, so he grabbed some blocks from a basket in the room to create a second sheepfold. We wondered about how coming to the table on Sundays was like being in the sheepfold; how coming to the Godly Play Room was like being in the sheepfold, and more. This is a story the children had seen almost every year since they were aged three, and yet on this day it was all new for them as they connected it to the psalm and their experiences in church.

Cheryl Minor and some of the children at All Saints' in Belmont reading Psalm 23 together and wondering with the material for the story called "Good Shepherd and World Communion."

Sometimes the wondering will seem "flat" to me. It is as if the children are just going through the motions. If it is a familiar story I might say, "I wonder what part you liked best when you were younger?" If it is a desert story they might say, "I'm sure it was the sand." I might follow up by asking, "Why do you think you liked the sand?" As they ponder what their younger self might have thought I will then say, "Now. You are much older. You have experienced so many new things since you were four and are so much more grown up. I wonder what your favorite part is now? I wonder what part you think is the most important now?" Remember the goal is to stimulate the creative process and start the scanning process for new insight and meaning.

Sharing Your Own Discoveries

A basic rule of thumb for Godly Play mentors is to facilitate wondering as opposed to leading it by sharing your own discoveries. This is very difficult, because as you watch and listen to the children, or even while telling the story yourself, new discoveries spring to life. Keeping them to yourself is a challenge, but we do so for good reason. As the storyteller you have real authority in the circle, and if you "say what you think," you risk shutting down the children's own discovery process. At the same time, however, if the storyteller never shares a personal discovery the unspoken lesson might be that discoveries are uncomfortable to share. Furthermore, the children could sense the anxiety the storyteller feels about sharing or not sharing a discovery, thus teaching the children that a new discovery makes one anxious. Berryman suggests:

> The best approach to sharing or not sharing new insights is to balance the risk of taking away the child's chance to make the discovery with the awareness that showing ourselves happily struck by a new insight reinforces the child's enjoyment of the creative process.[5]

I have found this is particularly important when working with children in middle and late childhood. They are much more keyed in to what the "teacher" is saying and doing, and often sharing an important discovery of your own is just what they need to feel it's safe to share what they are thinking. If you have fostered the sense that there is no right answer, then sharing your own thoughts is just part of all the possible ways of thinking about something. The same is true of the storyteller's attitude toward existential issues. Berryman writes:

> Experiences such as death, the threat of freedom, the need for meaning, or the unavoidable aloneness that marks us as human beings often raise the defenses of both adults and children . . . If we are repressing the

---

5. J. W. Berryman, *Godly Play: An Imaginative Approach to Religious Education* (Minneapolis, MN: Augsburg Press, 1991), 64.

awareness of existential limits in our own lives, we will communicate that to the children.[6]

I have been inspired by Berryman's book *Stories of God at Home: A Godly Play Approach* to connect my own journey through times of existential anxiety with the stories as a way of inviting the children to do the same. In *Stories of God at Home*, Berryman encourages parents, who are the storytellers, to look for openings to share their own family story with the stories of God. For example, when sharing the story of the journey of the Holy Family to Bethlehem during the season of Advent, a parent might share the story of when he or she went on a long journey. It might be a physical journey, but it could also be a journey of discovering his or her identity or purpose in life. I have seen this type of sharing stimulate older children to do the same kind of weaving of their own stories with the stories of the people of God, finding new language to use to think about what it is like to bump up against the existential limits in their own lives.

"Tuning Your Ears" for Relational Consciousness

I also want to highlight something that I learned when I spent the summer in residence at Children's Hospital in Dallas, Texas, where all the chaplains are trained to use Godly Play as a pastoral or spiritual intervention. One of my goals during my time at the hospital was to help the full-time chaplains and chaplain residents think about how they "chart." Just like the medical staff they are required to document their visits with patients, families, and staff in the medical charts. As part of a team of family support services, the chaplains work with the social workers and child life workers in the hospital. What is sometimes hard to discern is how the work of the chaplain is different from what these other professionals are doing for children and families. They were documenting what stories they were sharing and some of the things the children said, but I wondered if there were some more meaningful ways to write about what they were doing. I experimented with this when I wrote a verbatim—a word-for word-report of a visit I made with a family, complete with my analysis of the visit. By way of an analysis, I combed through the conversation to look for the ways the patient and the mom were expressing their spirituality, and how I was supporting it by what I did, said,

---

6. Ibid., 64.

or by what I didn't say or do. I used David Hay and Rebecca Nye's description of children's innate spirituality, what they call "relational consciousness"—an awareness of our relationships with the self, others, the transcendent, and the environment.[7] The conversation I had with the patient and her mother revealed this awareness in the patient in many ways. I also looked through the conversation for the times when the patient or her mother were grappling with existential issues such as aloneness, freedom, questions of meaning, and death, looking specifically for how my actions or words (I told a Godly Play story) helped give voice to these issues. The staff and residents in the pastoral care department took that work and began to think about how they might better chart these things.

I think this kind of thing could go far beyond the hospital and the work of chaplains. The goal of the chaplain is to support the child's spiritual life while they are being treated in the hospital, but of course all of us who love children want to do this whether they are in the hospital or not. We need to tune our ears to hear the child's spirituality and then set to work to find ways to support and nourish it so it can flourish. As we get better and better at hearing our children, we can find more and more opportunities to nurture that spirituality.

Introducing Side-by-Sides

Another way to open a story for children is to put another story beside it. If nothing much is happening with the wondering I will sometimes say, "Well, I wonder if another story can help us with this one?" I will then look around the room and pick a story to lay beside the one I told. For an example of how to do this, see Lesson 15 in *The Complete Guide to Godly Play,* Volume 3. In most instances I will pick one of the Core stories so it will be familiar to everyone. We will lay it out together and I'll remind the children of the details of the story. Then I will say, "Look at these stories together now. I wonder if we could take anything from this story and put it in this one (and vice versa)?"

---

7. D. Hay and R. Nye, *The Spirit of the Child,* rev. ed. (London: Jessica Kingsley Publishers 2006).

Cheryl Minor and some children from All Saints' in
Belmont working with two stories side-by-side.

One of my favorite memories is putting the story of the Holy Family (*The Complete Guide to Godly Play*, Volume 2, Lesson 4) next to the story of the Falling Apart (*The Complete Guide to Godly Play*, Volume 6, Lesson 1). One of the children in the circle placed Jesus right next to Adam and Eve. I said, "I wonder what he is saying to them?" She said, in almost a whisper, "I forgive you." There was another time when I put a Parable beside a Parable. After some interesting wondering a child said, "I think we need another one." I said, "Okay, go get the one you want." Before we were done, we had all six guiding Parables on the floor.

The idea of taking a story off the shelf and feeling ready to share it, even just in summary, can sometimes feel overwhelming to volunteers. For this reason, I try to schedule a few side-by-sides and help them prepare. Once they have had the experience of doing it, I find they are much more willing to try it spontaneously when the circle seems to need it.

Putting the Story Away or Leaving It Out?

The usual practice in Godly Play is that after the wondering, the storyteller carefully puts the story away, modeling for the children how to care for the materials. With children in middle and late childhood this is less important. They are already familiar with the way the story gets put back on the shelf for the most part. I still will usually put the story away, but sometimes I make the decision to leave the story where it is, particularly if some rich wondering has happened, or if we did a side-by-side lesson. Even if the work the children choose does not seem directly related to the lesson for the day and the work they did in the circle, the presence of the materials close by helps the scanning for new insight and understanding to continue, albeit in a nonverbal way.

Other Adaptations for Older Children

Some of the churches surveyed spoke of running out of dedicated space for Godly Play as the children grew older. They were forced to adapt an adult space for Godly Play on Sunday morning. One church described using a small meeting room for seventh and eighth graders (aged thirteen to fourteen) that had a large table for adults, with some shelves and cabinets surrounding it. They utilized the shelves and cabinets to store stories—a combination of Core Lessons and Extension and Enrichment Lessons. They are unable to do any response time, so they spend some extended time at the beginning asking about the children to share their "highs and lows" from the week. The wondering is more relaxed and deeper as there is no need to wrap things up in time for work. At the end the children bless each other before leaving the space.

Another church uses a more typical "youth space," filled with couches and chairs for their ninth to eleventh graders (aged fourteen to seventeen in the United States), a time when almost all churches stop using Godly Play. There is a small kitchenette where the children can fix themselves a cup of tea or hot chocolate. In this church they also focused on building relationships at the beginning, sharing their "highs and lows" from the week. After that the storyteller shares a story and leads them in an extended time of wondering. Sometimes they pull out the Bibles and read the lesson in several translations, comparing the differences. This group also works to discern a favorite story and plans a pilgrimage that is somehow connected to that story. The leader of this program shared that the deep wondering has been intense and thought provoking. She said, "Running Godly Play through secondary education has led to a huge increase in retention. Students no longer stop coming around aged thirteen. They come more often and hold each other to the task." She went on to say that she thinks continuing the program all the way through school sends an important message to the children. She said if you stop wondering about the stories at aged twelve, we send them the message that, "as an adult there isn't room for wondering . . . just when they need it most."

Conclusion

As I wrote this chapter my goal was to share both the joys of doing this work with children in middle and late childhood and the challenges. It is important to me that Godly Play practitioners have realistic expectations about this work. Yes, there are moments when the defenses of the children fall away, and deep sharing happens. But as I have tried to emphasize, often the creative process just gets going in the room. Afterall, most of us only have the typical "forty-five-minute Sunday school hour." One of the churches surveyed for this book mentioned that they were experimenting with lengthening the time of Godly Play for the older children. They said that the challenge was getting the parents to agree, but that the sessions were much better when they had a full seventy-five minutes. They wrote, "Those sessions were so amazing as nothing was rushed." Another program surveyed also spoke about lengthening the sessions, saying that the older children would often tell their parents to go get coffee before picking them up, or even just to go home without them so they could have more time in the room. The leader of the program said, "It was difficult to persuade them to leave the room and return to their parents." In this same program, the children resisted when they told them that they had to move on from Godly Play to "Bible class." They ended up "scrapping" Bible class and letting the children continue in Godly Play for as long as they needed. More often than not, however, lengthening the class time is not really possible. This means the work of insight, development, and articulation of the insight might be years in the making. I will say more about how those insights might get expressed in chapter eight. For now, let's turn our attention to response/work time.

CHAPTER 5

Response Time

They will respond to many things, trivial and profound, but the goal is for the children to begin to cope with their existential limits through expressive art or personal work with the lesson materials.[1]

The Lofty Goal and the Reality of Sunday Morning

The time after the lesson is sometimes called "Response time" and sometimes referred to as "work time" or the "work period." However, in Godly Play we believe that play is children's work, either alone or in small groups, thus the name "Godly Play." As they play with the lesson materials or engage in expressive art, we pray and hope that they can use this time to scan for insight, develop ideas, and cope with the existential limits of life made aware by the whole process of Godly Play. The limits are the four major boundaries that press in on us: death, the threat of freedom, the need for meaning, and our fundamental aloneness.[2] Both adults and children generally avoid thinking about these limits because they make us uncomfortable. Berryman suggests that

> . . . if there is a safe place and an appropriate language to cope with these limits then it is good to allow them into our consciousness and confront them so they can more explicitly frame our search for identity and ethical direction . . . During response time the children are encouraged to somersault into the awareness of their existential limits and use the Christian language to cope with them.[3]

This is a lofty goal for the forty-five-minute Sunday school hour and very difficult to measure. Many will ask, "Does Godly Play work?" I always want to

---

1. J. W. Berrryman, *Teaching Godly Play: How to Mentor the Spiritual Development of Children* ed. C. Minor (New York: Church Publishing, Inc., 2009), 66.
2. Ibid., 67.
3. J. W. Berryman, *Teaching Godly Play: How to Mentor the Spiritual Development of Children,* ed. C. Minor (New York: Church Publishing, Inc., 2009), 67.

know what they mean by "work." For most people it is something about church growth, that is, does it attract families and keep them coming. Others are thinking about the teachers. They want to know if it is easy to do. The real question is do we see children in Godly Play using the Christian language system artfully to cope with their existential limits. Another question might be, do we see them engaged in the creative process, scanning for insight and then developing and articulating that insight. My answer to these questions is that it is not always clear! Berryman writes:

> Most of the time we use a kind of knowing that attends to what is "out there" beyond us like a math problem, walking down a familiar street, or wondering about the Parable of the Good Shepherd. There is, however, always a subsidiary kind of knowing that is going on at the same time that is not the focal target of our attention. It is based on a lifetime of memories, feelings and other accumulations of experience, which provide the clues for understanding what our attention is focused on.[4]

The bottom line is that often we don't see any clear evidence that this work is going on. We see children drawing, coloring, working with a story, making something out of clay, and so on, but we do not see what is going on inside either consciously, or perhaps more importantly, unconsciously.

When my son was around eleven, I remember watching him play with his cousin one summer. They were building with Legos. This cousin had fairly recently lost his young father to a heart attack, and my son was very close to all the members of the family, so no doubt he was thinking about that and more. I watched him build three crosses out of the Legos. "Where Jesus died," he told me. Then he added a motorcycle with two figures on it. He told me it was him and his dad riding by and looking at the cross. While he didn't say anything explicitly about this, I can be almost sure that he was using the story he had heard in Godly Play about Jesus's death to cope with his existential anxiety about death—the death of his beloved uncle, and the idea that his own dad would die one day. I'm not sure what kind of work he chose in the Godly Play Room on the day they told him the story of Jesus's death. He might have made something kind of random out of clay (he

---

4. Ibid., 67.

always loved to work with the clay) or chose to play in the desert box with some of the other children. The teachers and parents involved might have been tempted to think that Godly Play was not "working" for him because he didn't make something that looked connected to the lesson. But clearly it was working. After this experience with my son, and many others like it, I grew far less worried about what I was seeing or not seeing during work time and began to trust that there was much more going on than I could see with my eyes.

Part of why we do not always see the fruits of this work in the room is the lack of time, as I have already suggested. That is why I called this section a lofty goal and the reality of Sunday morning. The time we have them in the room is generally too short to see the whole of the creative process. We start the process by giving them both the language and a sense of wonder about it all. We need to trust that they have a lifetime to work on the rest. One of the young adults we interviewed for this book spoke of how the practice of wondering, something he said he had been doing "his whole life," was something he most cherished about his time in Godly Play.

Choosing Work

The children in middle childhood (aged six to nine) will often get the stories off the shelves to work with. They enjoy retelling the stories to themselves, mixing stories together, or making up their own stories. I have found, however, that older children (aged nine to twelve) are less likely to do that. My guess is that they worry about looking silly to their peers as they "play" with the artifacts. For this reason, I often place books and puzzles under a lesson as a kind of extension material. This is both a popular and a less risky way to keep exploring a story they have heard in the circle. Godly Play Resources has some recommended "materials to deepen your shelves" in their shop, and you will find an annotated list of recommended print materials in Appendix D, p. 131.

Children can also choose to work with art materials in the room. Just as with the younger children, I make sure there is plenty of paper, markers, and colored pencils on the shelves. But in addition, I rotate in other more sophisticated materials. I make sure to rotate these materials on and off the shelves throughout the year to keep from overwhelming the children with too many choices. Above all else, the materials need to be of a high quality and more sophisticated than what you might find in the preschool room. Below is a list of some of the types of materials I keep on hand, rotating them on and off the shelf throughout the year:

- White Paper
- Construction Paper
- Markers
- Colored Pencils
- Poster Paints
- Watercolor Paints
- Oil Pastels
- Clay
- Glitter Glue
- Craft Sticks (plain and colored)

Other ideas shared by Godly Play Trainers include keeping a request list so the children can request materials. The person who suggested this said, "I had second graders request things they could build, '"like with wood and nails'" and safety goggles!" Another trainer mentioned having a brass polishing station in the room.

Children in Middle and Late Childhood and Expressive Art

Young children often use expressive art as a way of communicating how they are feeling. As children get older, they begin to rely more on their verbal abilities to express their ideas and understandings of the world around them.[5] Children in later elementary grades have a growing interest in achieving realism in their work. Children in this age range are also increasingly less comfortable with artistic risk-taking and experimentation and are more sensitive to perceived criticism about their artistic abilities. At the same time, the children in this age group are drawn to the art materials. I believe this is because there are very few places during their busy schedules when they are given permission to work with their hands without a product being forced. The freedom to do "whatever their hands want to do" is

---

5. K. M. Edens and E. F. Potter, "Promoting Conceptual Understanding Through Pictorial Representation, *Studies in Art Education* 42, no. 3 (2001): 214–233.

exciting. For these reasons and more I have found it is important to have a mix of options on the art shelves—some that are very open, and others that are perhaps less risky for those who are more self-conscious.

Less Risky Art Choices for Children in Middle and Late Childhood

Sewing Work

Children use yarn, plastic needles and burlap to make designs. Purchase a few yards of burlap and cut it into large square pieces. Put the burlap on a tray with some plastic embroidery hoops next to it. The children can use plastic needles and yarn to create designs on the burlap, using the embroidery hoops as a frame. Yarn of different colors is rolled into balls and placed into small mason jars or baby food jars. You can punch a hole in the cover of the jar through which to pull the yarn. When you first introduce this work the children will need some help threading the needle and some modeling about how to push the yarn in and out of the burlap. Another alternative is to purchase small plastic frames in different shapes. The children can then use colorful shoelaces to create a design.

Sewing work materials.

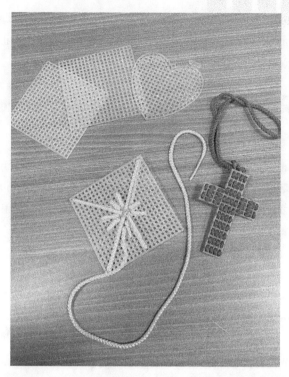

Sewing work using plastic frames and shoelaces.

Push-Pin Work

For this work children use large push pins to "punch out" a design they make or use one of the designs I have on the shelf. Place some large push pins on a small tray. Cut pieces of thick foam bulletin board, small enough to put on a small clipboard. I put out pieces of shiny craft paper on a tray beside push pins. On another tray I put copies of Christian symbols or other seasonal images on plain paper, cut to fit on the clipboard. The children choose some craft paper and clip it to the clipboard. Then they pick a symbol and clip that to the board on top of the craft paper. With the push pin they "punch out" the design. When they are done, they can put the punched-out design in a window to catch the light, or use the punched-out image to create a rubbing of the same design, using a crayon or marker. To do a rubbing they place the punched-out design on a flat surface (the back side is the rough side) and put a piece of paper over it. Then they grab a crayon and color the whole paper. As they do the image will appear. It helps to have some crayons with paper peeled off so you can use the side of the crayon instead of the tip.

Push-pin work materials.

Push-pin work in progress.

Bead Work

There are many options for bead work. You can have small beads that children thread onto pipe cleaners, yarn, or embroidery thread. Large wooden beads can be threaded onto shoelaces to create prayer beads. The children could also make their own beads out of clay, paint them, and then thread them onto colorful shoelaces.

Materials for bead work.

Mosaic Work

The mosaic work in my room includes some examples of a mosaic (a friend brought me back a few from her trip to the Holy Land), thick paper to use when creating a mosaic, and materials to make a design on the paper (small tiles that can be glued in any shape). Some craft stores will have "stick-on" tiles (paper peels off the back side revealing a sticky side), so you do not need glue.

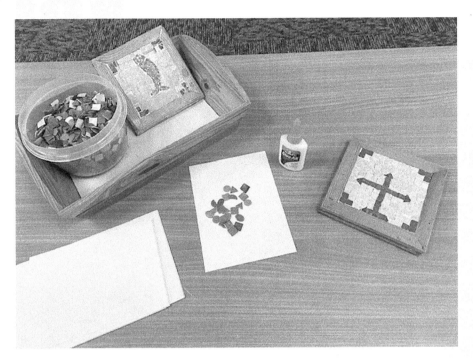

Materials for mosaic work.

Architectural Blocks

I will rotate in a basket of high-quality architectural blocks for the children to use to build with.

Mono-chromatic Building Blocks

I will rotate in a basket of small, brown building blocks for the children to build with. One year a group of children worked hard together to make an Ark out of the blocks, while another group recreated the Temple.

Some children working with the building blocks to rec-
reate the Temple during work time.

Kindness Rocks

Several years ago, there was a movement across the country called kindness rocks.
People would paint small rocks with inspirational messages and then place them
around their town for people to find. I keep a basket of rocks in our room for the
children to paint in just the same way. It helps to paint them blue or white as can-
vas for their design or message. Afterwards you can spray them with some protec-
tive coating so they can be placed outside of the church. We even have a sign in
our garden inviting passersby to take a rock if they find it inspiring.

Kindness rocks painted by some children at All
Saints' in Belmont, Massachusetts.

Puzzles

My room for older children also has some beautiful puzzles that extend or enrich
the stories on the shelves. You can find large floor puzzles of the Ark and the Flood
for example. If they have lots of pieces, it can become a multi-week project for a
small group of children. Puzzle mats work well to use as a base so you can roll up
the puzzle between times.

Outreach Projects

As children move into late childhood in particular, they are often interested in
doing something to help others. I have patterns and materials for them to make
paper versions of the Parable of the Good Shepherd for the local children's hospital. What you will need are: green file folders, brown strips of construction paper
for the sheepfold, dark construction paper rocks for the dangerous places, blue
construction paper water (all of that gets glued to the inside of the file folder—see
picture), small package of crayons (the chaplain leaves these with the child to color

the figures after the story is told), black and white patterns for the figures (these are available at Godly Play Resources as a digital download so you can make as many copies as you want—https://store.godlyplayfoundation.org/products /he336cp2), an envelope to put all the figures and crayons in (we glue them to the outside of the envelope), a label that says "the Good Shepherd" (see photo), and glue sticks. I also have materials to make cards for friends or family members on the shelf.

Materials for making paper versions of the Parable of
the Good Shepherd to be used in hospitals.

Seasonal Projects

At Christmastime I will sometimes put materials on the shelf to make Christmas ornaments. As Easter approaches, I make sure to have plenty of wooden Easter eggs for the children to decorate. Just a hint about the wooden eggs: It helps to spray paint them all white. I have also found that colored pencils or thin markers work best if the children are making intricate designs.

Encouraging Prayerful Response Time

I have begun to include a "meditation corner" in all of my Godly Play Rooms—a place where a child can go to be intentionally quiet during response time. It includes a comfortable chair and a low table or shelf in a quiet corner of the room.

The meditation shelf in one of the Godly Play Rooms
at All Saints' in Belmont, Massachusetts.

I try to change the things in the corner from time to time, but here is brief list of some of the things I put on it:

- "Zen Drawing Board": A Zen Drawing Board—sometimes called a Buddha Board is inspired by the Zen idea of living in the moment. You can purchase them online or in most toy stores. You can also make one yourself. I have seen lots of posts about it on Pinterest. How does it work? You simply paint on the surface with water and your creation will come to life. Then, as the water slowly evaporates, your art will magically disappear.
- Mandalas to color, including beautiful pens or colored pencils for the children to use.

- Books (see complete list of recommended books in Appendix D, p. 131): I have some lovely books about centering prayer for children, Jerome Berryman's book called *Silence*, books about praying in color, and more.
- Music: I have some CDs of nature sounds, classical music, and more. There are a few personal CD players for the children to use as they work on a mandala, and so on.

In the rooms for older children, I will sometimes pull something off that shelf in place of the usual story or after the story to encourage some prayerful time during response time. We will read the book together or talk about what they could do with the object (pray in color, write to God, and so on). This is simply one way to introduce some different ways of praying to the children—giving them some tools to use during response time or when they are at home. There are a few books out there that I have found particularly helpful:

- *Journey to the Heart: Centering Prayer for Children*, by Frank X. Jelenek.
  — This book explains centering prayer and then lays out a step-by-step process that is easy to use with a group.
- *Praying in Color*, by Sybil Macbeth.
  — She has one that she has written just for children that introduces this practice. I also love the coloring books that go with this series and will at times invite the children to choose one of the pages to use during response time.
- *Writing to God*, by Rachel Hackenberg.
  — This book has a number of activities to get children started using a prayer journal. Each child has a journal in our room, so sometimes I'll ask them to go get them and spend a few moments trying one of the activities as a group. Categories include: writing prayers that use your five senses; writing to God about your feelings; writing to God about nature; writing to God about ordinary events in your life; writing prayers of gratitude. Children can write or draw about these things.
- *Silence,* by Jerome Berryman.
  — Jerome Berryman's children's book about silence is also a wonderful tool to help children discover silence—the stillness from within. At least once a year I will read this book to the children, in place of the usual story, and wonder with the children about it. Afterwards the book "lives" in the meditation corner for the children to explore on their own.

When Response Time Is Not Working

I would be remiss if I didn't share with you that at times the work time just doesn't seem to be working. I had a group of children a few years ago that exhibited some very disrespectful behavior. It climaxed with one child putting a "kick me" sign on the adult volunteer covering for me one week. I finally sat down with the parents and suggested that the children who were struggling take a break from work time. They were welcome to come in and hear the story, but after that I would be sending them down to sit with their parents in the church for a few weeks. I hoped a break from the cycle would help. I also enlisted the parents' help in adding some materials to the shelves that might interest them in a fresh way. After about a month I gathered them together and showed them the new things in the room. They were all about eleven years old, so we talked with some seriousness about what work time was really for—a chance to think about the stories and other things happening in their lives on their own, or to talk quietly with their peers about these things. I said that the fooling around they were doing was best kept for coffee hour. They agreed and seemed ready to try again. Things were much better after that. They were especially glad to be able to stay for the feast, which we will talk about in the next chapter. One of the churches surveyed shared that when a child's behavior becomes particularly disrespectful, she will create a covenant of behavior with the child and sometimes parents/caregivers before they come to Sunday school.

Conclusion

In the surveys we heard a great deal about the joys of watching the older children engage deeply with materials during the storytelling and during response time. One of those surveyed said it well when she wrote:

> Some days response time is quiet and peaceful. Some days it is decidedly not. We have to meet the children where they are and flow with what they need. But I am firm that response time remains non-directed.

One respondent told the story about a fifth grader (aged ten) who picked up the wolf after the Good Shepherd parable and said, "Adults are so worried about and afraid of the wolf . . . they spend all their times preparing to fight it and forget about the Good Shepherd. They leave his values behind." Another fifth grader whose parents were in the middle of a divorce sat outside of the classroom one week silently crying. As she looked in at the circle of children silently staring at a story she said, "This silence is so special to me right now." This same leader said that she thinks that Godly Play "comes to fruition" when children enter middle and late childhood. She said,

> The questions they ask of one another during wondering time, the openness of their sharing, the way they use the pieces of the story to make a point (e.g. lifting up the wolf from one parable and putting it in the other to ask where evil comes from), the maturing into contemplative silence during the stories, the long, complex group projects during work time—all of this has been building from an early age and comes into its own in older children.

In the chapter on the environment, we talked a great deal about the importance of the Godly Play environment, and I believe this is very much connected to how the older children engage during work time. For example, at my church we recently did a beautiful renovation of a Godly Play Room. We knocked down a wall, creating a spacious space filled with light. I have noticed the older children in the room paying closer attention to all the extra materials I have placed on the lower shelves just for them—books, puzzles, and so on. When we first entered the room (we were away for over a year due to the Covid-19 pandemic), the oldest children would simply wander around the room very slowly during work time. It was as if they were seeing some of the things on the shelf for the first time. I saw one middle-schooler settle down on the floor with a book about gargoyles that "lives" under the lesson about "the Church" (*The Complete Guide to Godly Play*, Volume 8, Lesson 14). That same day another middle-schooler explored the "meditation corner" and found a book about things that scare children (*What Scares Me and What I Do About It* by Jeff Kunkel). She came over to where I was sitting and we looked at it together, talking about how we were also scared of some of the same things. Much of what is there was in the room before, but the room was smaller and so things were simply harder to see. It underlines for me how important the space is for all aspects of the Godly Play method, but especially the response time.

We will now turn our attention to the next part of the session, "the feast." Jerome Berryman often says, "Never skip the feast!"

CHAPTER 6

The Feast

There's a big difference between a feast and snack. You might have the same food to eat, but that is not what counts. What is important is how you feel about it. Sometimes the food is little but the feelings are big. It's the big feelings that make a feast.[1]

Jerome Berryman is often quoted as saying, "Never skip the feast," and yet, many churches who use Godly Play do! There are several arguments made in defending this choice, the first being the lack of time. As I mentioned in previous chapters, the classic "forty-five-minute Sunday school hour" is the norm in many places, and to make matters worse, children often arrive late. We love the stories. The children look forward to response time. Something has to get left out sometimes, and most often it is the feast. In many liturgical churches the children join their families in the church after Godly Play for Holy Communion. People ask, "Can't that take the place of the feast?" In other places there is a tradition of fellowship after Sunday school which includes all kinds of fun food. Can't that take the place of the feast? In this chapter I will argue that these things are definitely connected to what happens during the feast in a Godly Play session but cannot replace that important moment for a number of reasons.

The Benefits of Feast Mirror the Benefits of Family Meal-Time

Research indicates there are real benefits to sharing a meal together as a family.[2] A study conducted by Berge et al. (2013) found that

> The family meal affords benefits such as positive nutritional habits, trust-building, connecting, parent modeling, and teaching. During the school-aged

1. J. W. Berryman, *Godly Play: An Imaginative Approach to Religious Education* (Minneapolis, MN: Augsburg Press, 1991), 39.
2. J. M. Berge, C. Hoppmann, C. Hanson, D. Neumark-Sztainer, "Perspectives about Family Meals from Single-Headed and Dual-Headed Households: A Qualitative Analysis," *Journal of the Academy of Nutrition & Dietetics*, 113 (2013), 1632–1639. doi:10.1016/j.jand.2013.08.023.

years, families can support children's development of health behaviors and family routines.[3]

Studies show this is a regular part of the lives of young children, but that it gets increasingly rare as children move into middle and late childhood.[4] The reasons are obvious. As young as age four children begin group sports, music lessons, and dance lessons, among other things, making the family's schedule packed with car rides, as well as hastily prepared and hastily eaten meals. This could mean that feast time in Godly Play is one of the rare moments in the week when children sit and enjoy some food and conversation with other people. It is an opportunity to practice the skill of listening to others or taking turns sharing and talking.

As the children move into middle and late childhood, they can also take on more responsibility vis-à-vis the feast. While younger children can pass out the napkins and the food, the older children can be responsible for preparing the feast. This is what we hope will happen at home around meals as well, so it is good to support that in Godly Play.

Praying with Children in Middle and Late Childhood

As children move into middle and late childhood, they become more self-conscious about praying out loud. While we often sing our prayers with the younger children, older children are sometimes insecure about their singing voices, especially with their peers. We also ask the younger children to pray out loud, perhaps naming one thing they are thankful for this week. With the younger children we always make it optional, saying a child can pray quietly to themselves or even say "pass" as we move around the circle. This can quickly turn into something more negative with the older children as they watch what their peers do very carefully and will follow along. Suddenly as you go around the circle inviting prayer, no one is praying out loud. When this happens, it is my cue to introduce some new ways of praying.

---

3. Ibid., 1632.
4. M. E. Eisenberg, R. E. Olson, D. Neumark-Sztainer, M. Story, L. H. Bearinger, "Correlations Between Family Meals and Psychosocial Well-being Among Adolescents," *The Archives of Pediatrics & Adolescent Medicine*, 158, no. 8 (2004): 792–796. doi:10.1001/archpedi.158.8.792.

- Asking for specific prayer requests.

  I will often ask the children if there is something big coming up that I could pray for, for example a test at school, a soccer game, a project that is due. We will go around the circle and each child will name one thing. I will then pray for all those things and finish by thanking God for our time together in Godly Play and for the food. I change it up by asking different questions each week, such as asking if they know anyone who is sick or sad who needs prayer. I have noticed that since starting this practice, many more children are coming up for private prayer during worship. It is our practice to offer healing prayer and other sorts of private prayer in the side-chapel during communion. The children take advantage of this opportunity more than the adults, coming up for prayer for a sick grandparent, a test they have coming up, and more. This is, I believe, because they are learning to pray for these sorts of things in Godly Play.

- Confession

  Some weeks we do a kind of "embodied confession," which I learned from Caroline Fairless in her book *Children at Worship: Congregations in Bloom* (2000). She writes about placing a basket of rocks in each pew.[5] Children and adults are invited to pick a rock to hold in their hands. They are asked to think of something they are sorry for—perhaps something they did, a person they hurt, and so on. They are directed to think about placing that "on their rock," using their imaginations, of course. They then place the rocks in a bowl, maybe even the baptismal font, and as the priest gives the absolution of sins she pours water over the rocks, washing them clean. We do this in the Godly Play Room, using the bowl from the baptismal lesson (*The Complete Guide to Godly Play*, Volume 3, Lesson 8).

Community Building

The feast is also a key part of building a sense of community for the children. At Godly Play training I often hear people lament about the lack of deep wondering in their circles. Younger children are quick to offer their thoughts, but older children

---

5. C. Fairless, *Children at Worship: Congregations in Bloom* (New York: Church Publishing, Inc., 2000), 87.

often sit back to wait and see what their peers might say. This hesitancy begets more hesitancy as few feel confident enough to break the silence. This is not all bad. The silence is often "heavy" with deep thoughts. I often ask adults to imagine what it might be like to be asked to respond to a sermon in front of the whole church. It would be uncomfortable for most people. However, as the children get to know each other in more casual times, such as the feast, "wondering" out loud can become less daunting.

Children who have been together for several years really look forward to both response time and feast time as a chance to catch up with their friends. One difficulty is when they start visiting with their friends and the feast sounds more like a cocktail hour than a family meal. The mentors need to set some boundaries around this time, just as we do with the rest of the session, to encourage respectful turn-taking and good listening. Sometimes I will introduce a topic to help everyone feel comfortable. I'll ask about projects at school saying, "What are you all working on at school right now? Are there any big projects happening?" Several of our survey respondents spoke of how much the children enjoy sharing "news" during this time. One person said, "Feast time seems even more important for the older children. If the circle is formed, they share a lot . . . more I think than they would with school friends."

Preparation for Worship

The Godly Play session mirrors the liturgy of most traditions (see the chart below to see a comparison of worship in a congregation with a Godly Play session).

Gathering	Crossing the Threshold & Making a Circle
Reading from Scripture	The Story or Lesson for the Day
Sermon	The Wondering
Creeds & Prayers	Response Time
Holy Communion	The Feast
Blessing & Dismissal	Blessing

Not all traditions include Holy Communion every week, but it is a regular part of congregational life. Berryman writes: "Holy Communion is of fundamental importance to all Christian people, even the Quakers who reject symbols but find communion in silence 'after the manner of friends' to be something they cannot do without." [6] The feast is not Holy Communion, but the feelings it engenders are similar in the way that the community gathers to pray and share some simple food together. It helps to slow things down and be present to God and to one another. Including the feast each week reinforces the ritual the children will be a part of in congregational worship, as do the specific lessons on Holy Communion in the room.

What Will We Eat?

Younger children enjoy crackers, small cookies, and the like for their feast. Older children still enjoy those foods, but I recommend appealing to their more sophisticated tastebuds by adding some more varied options to the feast. Invite volunteers to bake breakfast muffins to share at the feast time or include breakfast bars as a choice. One Godly Play mentor I know decided to serve a different type of bread as the feast each week. He came up with over thirty types of bread—pita bread, focaccia, matzo, French bread, sourdough bread, wheat bread, pumpernickel bread, raisin bread, and so on (some he purchased, others he baked). At holiday times consider a holiday-themed feast. Every year for Pentecost I made sure to include something red. Red velvet cupcakes were a hit as were the little red candies called "Red Hots." One year we had strawberries and red apple slices.

The Blessing

At every training Godly Play mentors are encouraged to say goodbye to each child at the end of the session and to give "a word of blessing." This can simply be something you noticed that day about the child, "I saw you working with the blue paint today," or "I saw you sharing the desert box with _____ today," or "Thank you for helping with the feast today." That moment of intimacy can become more awkward with the older children, especially when they are new and do not know the adults in the room well. Still, it is worth it to take a moment with each of them and say goodbye. It communicates to them that you really "see" them and care for them. I recommend you keep it light and friendly, wishing them

---

6. J. W. Berryman, *Teaching Godly Play: How to Mentor the Spiritual Development of Children*, ed. C. Minor (New York: Church Publishing, Inc., 2009), 92.

a good week and thanking them for coming and joining in the session. If something special happened, you can mention that as well.

Conclusion

Do not skip the feast! It is important on many levels. Most important for the children in middle and late childhood is the opportunity it gives to build community and safety. It is only when the children feel known and loved that they can open themselves up to new learning and find ways to express all that they are feeling during this crucial time of development.

We will now turn our attention to the nurturers, and how they can be enlisted to help make Godly Play work well for the children in middle and late childhood.

CHAPTER 7

Nurturing the Nurturers

One needs to stay close to children to grow as a Godly Play teacher (or parent) . . . this "growth" is not like the growth of an arm or leg that stays the same but gets larger. It involves a rhythm of exploring, integrating and confirming over a cycle of three years (and more). [1]

In this chapter I want to talk about three different kinds of nurture, all of which are essential when doing Godly Play with any age, but especially with children in middle and late childhood. First, you need to carefully nurture the volunteers who are being called to do this work with the older children. Second, you need to reach out to the parents and nurture them in such a way as to enlist them as partners in this work. Finally, I urge you to find ways to nurture yourself.

Nurturing Your Volunteers

Training is the most important and at the same time the most challenging part of nurturing volunteer Godly Play mentors. It is challenging because of the time and expense involved. Churches struggle to get volunteers for all sorts of things, but the time commitment involved in serving as a Godly Play mentor can seem overwhelming for many. Learning a story "by heart" feels impossible. Committing to be in church on a regular basis feels like too much when so much else is crying for our Sunday morning attention (brunch with our friends, hikes in the mountains, children who need shuttling to sports, parties, and more). A request to attend a three-day training in preparation for the work also sounds impossible, especially if you are being asked to pay for it yourself! My advice is to begin small. Bring in a Godly Play Trainer to do a ninety-minute training one evening or attend one online. People will begin to see that training is meaningful and even retreat-like. The Godly Play Foundation now offers door-person training online regularly and it is a great way to get volunteers started on their Godly Play journey. A half day is

---

1. J. W. Berryman, *Teaching Godly Play: How to Mentor the Spiritual Development of Children,* ed. C. Minor (New York: Church Publishing, Inc., 2009), 129.

the next step, then a full day, leading up to the idea that a three-day training might just be possible and could even be exciting.

It is important to get people to trainings because there are a lot of things you can learn from a lecture, but Godly Play is best learned from the inside out. This is what we do at Godly Play Training. Within a circle facilitated by a Godly Play Trainer, participants experience and learn Godly Play stories, practices, and theology in a retreat-like setting. Our Trainers will deepen your understanding of children's spirituality, lead you on an exploration of the fundamentals of the prepared environment, and give you the tools needed to support the children you mentor. It can be both intense and deeply restful. You will leave feeling more prepared to do this work and feel spiritually refreshed.

As the children grow, the mentors need to grow too. I always recommend putting your most experienced Godly Play mentors in the room with the children who are more experienced. They will be the most equipped to move to the next level with the children. At the same time, they will need extra support as the children develop and begin to push back at the process. This might mean regular times to gather and debrief the experience of leading the sessions, and time to work with the stories in a group of adults before presenting them to the children. It might also mean returning to the three-day Core training to experience all of it with fresh eyes. The Godly Play Foundation also offers enrichment days, and a three-day Advanced Training, which includes more teaching on the spiral curriculum, experience with Extension, Enrichment, and Synthesis lessons, and a time to share case studies from the experiences the mentors are having in their circles. Many of the churches we surveyed who are successfully using Godly Play with children in middle and late childhood reported that their storytellers had been to both a Core and Advanced Godly Play training.

The Godly Play mentors also need encouragement from the clergy leading the parish. The best way to accomplish this is by getting clergy trained. Even just attending an online introduction to Godly Play will go a long way to equipping them to be supportive in meaningful ways. The clergy may never help lead a Godly Play circle, but they need to understand what is involved in the method, including and most especially the importance of the prepared environment. They will become advocates for providing money in the annual budget for training and resources if they understand why it is needed. Finally, they can speak to parents as someone informed by training when questions arise, or when there is some resistance in the community about doing Godly Play with the older children.

Many of the Godly Play mentors in my church have been doing this work with me for over twenty years. They started when their own children were in the program. Now their children are grown and living on their own. Still, they continue the work. They are not just volunteers, "doing their time" teaching Sunday school, but are engaged in a ministry that not only serves the children but feeds their souls as well. At the end of Dr. Berryman's 1991 book, *Godly Play: A Way of Religious Education*, he writes about how Godly Play keeps open the opportunity for the true self to emerge in childhood, but that is also a way for the adults engaged in this ministry to return to where they began and "begin to grow again."[2]

One of the churches in the survey we conducted spoke specifically about how much the storytellers in their church loved the work with the children. The leader of the program wrote:

> We—and I speak for the other storytellers in my church too—find that we learn so much from working with the stories and listening to the children's wondering—we usually debrief, where we have the opportunity to wonder too. The program is addictive and the more we do, the more we want to do.

Nurturing the Parents

No one will dispute how important parenting is to a child's spiritual growth and well-being. Research has shown that most adolescents will follow in their parents' religious traditions (or lack thereof). "Most teenagers and their parents may not realize it, but a lot of research in the sociology of religion suggests that the most important social influence in shaping young people's religious lives is the religious life modeled and taught to them by their parents," observe Christian Smith and Melinda Denton in their 2005 book, *Soul Searching: The Religious and Spiritual Lives of American Teenagers.* John Westerhoff, renowned Christian educator,

---

2. J. W. Berryman, *Godly Play: An Imaginative Approach to Religious Education* (Minneapolis, MN: Augsburg Fortress, 1991), 158.

famously said that faith is more caught than it is taught.[3] Many years ago, Robert Wuthnow conducted a study at Princeton University that speaks to this (1999).[4] He interviewed students at Princeton involved in the religious life of the university in some way. He wanted to know what was causing them to reach for God at this time in their lives, when many fall away from church. He thought they might speak of going to church, or family activities such as Bible study or devotions. He did hear some of that, but what he heard the most was that these young adults reaching for God were doing so because they had seen it modeled for them by the adults in their lives—parents, grandparents, aunts, uncles, and so on. They spoke of Dad, sitting in his chair reading the Bible. They remembered Grandma getting up every day and walking to church to attend Mass. They didn't read the Bible with Dad or attend Mass with Grandma, not daily anyway, but they saw these trusted adults reaching for God. It was meaningful for them, and so they decided it must be trustworthy, and they, in turn, were reaching for God as well. What this means for me is that we need to not only pay attention to how we are feeding children when we talk about nurturing their spiritual well-being, but it is equally important to consider carefully how we are feeding adults.

No doubt they are getting some spiritual nourishment out of worship, although there can sometimes be a bit of dissonance between what happens in worship and what happens in a Godly Play Room. Depending on the style of the clergy, for example, the sermons alone can be more didactic in nature than open to wondering and mystery. I recommend offering some Godly Play sessions for the parents as a way to introduce them to the method. Rebecca McClain's book *Graceful Nurture* outlines a number of "courses" someone could lead in a congregation for adults, in the "style of Godly Play."[5] There is a twelve-week course using Godly Play stories to prepare adults for Baptism or Confirmation. There is a six-week course that introduces parents to the Godly Play method. There is another twelve-week course that uses Godly Play lessons for newcomers to a church. Finally, there is an outline of a retreat that uses Godly Play stories as the centerpiece.

---

3. J. Westerhoff, *Will Our Children Have Faith?* rev. ed. (New York: Morehouse Publishing, 2012).

4. R. Wuthnow, *Growing Up Religious: Christians and Jews and Their Journeys of Faith* (Boston: Beacon Press, 1999).

5. R. McClain, *Graceful Nurture: Using Godly Play with Adults* (New York: Church Publishing Inc., 2017).

Another important resource is Jerome Berryman's book *Stories of God at Home: A Godly Play Approach.*[6] This book, written explicitly for parents, describes how parents can use six of our beloved Godly Play stories at home during important times of the year such as Advent and Christmas, Lent, Easter, and Pentecost. There is a chapter about using the story of Creation with your children at home, or when you are in a beloved vacation spot. The Parable of the Good Shepherd is also shared as a story to be used anytime, but especially when a family is going through a hard time (suffering, illness, grief, and so on). What is unique about the *Stories of God at Home* approach is that families are encouraged to weave their own family stories with these pivotal stories of God. The Center for the Theology of Childhood for the Godly Play Foundation has developed a number of resources for leaders to use as they seek to introduce this approach to parents, including demonstration videos, guides, and more. Godly Play Resources has also developed smaller versions of the lessons for use at home, including do-it-yourself kits to make the materials more affordable. Visit www.godlyplayfoundation.org/at-home to find these resources.

Much of what we learned about supporting families during the Covid-19 pandemic should continue to guide us as we work with parents going forward. Before the pandemic, Godly Play was, of course, most commonly part of a Sunday morning "church school" program or as part of religious education in a school setting. When the pandemic hit, everything had to change. For children to continue experiencing Godly Play, it had to happen on screens or in small family settings, and for most that meant that the adults in the home were involved either as participants or tech support. The expansion of the Godly Play circle to include caregivers seemed in many ways a uniquely positive part of pandemic life.

In a survey sent to parents, many spoke of finding a new way to connect with their children as they shared the experience of Godly Play. One mother commented that the Godly Play experiences stimulated "spiritual conversations" that she wished they had before the pandemic. Another said that after this experience, she believes that Godly Play has value for all generations. She wrote, "I'd love to see

---

6. J. W. Berryman, *Stories of God at Home: A Godly Play Approach* (New York: Church Publishing, Inc., 2018).

the approach be introduced and explained to our whole congregation and all ages invited to participate somehow." She wrote,

> I joined in their play and some family sessions our storyteller ran. It was a huge blessing to me. I think the spiritual life of our household was enhanced by the practice. Since it stopped, our spiritual life has been much poorer as a family.

Several of those surveyed and interviewed spoke of how the experience of Godly Play at home helped them to think about their faith not just on Sunday mornings but throughout the week. This study highlights the importance of equipping parents to join their child's spiritual journey in a way formed by Godly Play. The families who lived through this experience are now equipped with new ways to wonder together and share the language of the stories. Learning a new language is much easier if it is spoken at home! Going forward, faith communities must continue to assist caregivers in understanding the language of Godly Play and learning how to wonder with their children.

Nurturing Yourself

As a leader in the church, whether you are leading Godly Play or something else, it is important to take time to nurture yourself. I am not talking about the kind of stuff you read in the latest self-help book or blog, although much of that is good to consider. I am, instead, talking about finding time to feed your own Godly Play journey. I often tell people that I train that they need to "find their tribe." What I mean is that they need to find others who are passionate about this work and spend time together. At the center of that time is sharing stories and wondering together. We know from experience that the more you immerse yourself in the stories and do your own work of wondering about what they really mean for you personally, the better prepared you will be to hold space for children to do this work.

I have also learned as a seasoned storyteller, that even if I think I know the stories, I need to give myself the time to adequately prepare to lead the session. This means getting down on the floor with the materials and practicing, yes, but also spending some time with the language. I will create a "doodle" of a story to help me pray with important phrases or questions the story raises in me. Some record the story and then spend the week listening to it as they walk, or cook, for example. I had one teacher who found it helped her to write the story down longhand. Find the way that works for you! All of this helps the story to take shape inside of you, so that when you sit and tell it to children it comes from an authentic place inside of you. It also becomes so deeply rooted in you that the disruptions that are part of this work, especially when working with older children, do not "throw you off"; you become more adept at stopping to address the disruption, and return to the story with little effort.

Conclusion

Spend some time thinking about all three aspects of nurture described in this chapter and do a kind of audit of how things are going now, and what your goals are going forward.

1. How are you currently nurturing your volunteers? What is working? What would you like to try this year? How can you provide the important training needed to do this work?

2. How are you currently nurturing the parents in your community? What is working? What do you think you might try to add this year?

3. How are you nurturing yourself? What is missing for you as you do this work?

CHAPTER 8

Why Do It?

Knowing God is not something one can accomplish in a once-and-for-all way. There is no stopping place, no finish line, in time and space. . . . One does not become fed up with the desire for the spiritual quest . . . as God continues to call us forward.[1]

This book describes many challenges in doing Godly Play with children in middle and late childhood. Some of those challenges are related to the children themselves (chapter one), some are about the resources needed to do this work well (chapter two). Other challenges are connected to the time required to prepare for the work (training), or the adult caregivers and/or leaders in the congregation (clergy) who struggle to understand how Godly Play does continue to nurture their children as they move into middle and late childhood (chapter seven). I have worked to lift up solutions to all of these challenges, but none of them are easy fixes; all of the solutions require a kind of tenacity and time that might seem overwhelming or even impossible in today's church context. If this is so challenging, why do it? In this chapter I hope to answer that question, both from the perspective of those who research children's spiritual lives and by asking the children themselves. To that end, let me begin with a story.

When my son was in the eighth grade (aged thirteen and fourteen), he was assigned a variety of writing projects throughout the school year by his language arts teacher. There were essays about his personal life, book reviews, poems, and more. At the end of the year, these different pieces were collected to create a portfolio of his work. The very last assignment was to give his portfolio a title and write an introduction. This was due on a Monday, so during the weekend he worked on it. Now I should back up and tell you that I was usually his homework helper, even in the eighth grade. He had a learning disorder, and often needed some "scaffolding" to get through his assignments, especially writing assignments. However,

---

1. J. W. Berryman, *Godly Play: An Imaginative Approach to Religious Education* (Minneapolis, MN: Augsburg Press, 1991), 157.

this time I was out of town, so he worked on his own. When I returned home on Sunday evening, he asked me to look at what he had written. Here is an excerpt:

> Creating my Literary Portfolio was an enjoyable experience. Whenever there was a time when there wasn't much work to be done, it was great to have a portfolio piece to do. These pieces filled in the cracks in the year and allowed my creativity to flow. I learned that I loved writing about stories and memories. It's almost like looking through an old picture book filled with good times. My title, "End of the Beginning, Beginning of the End," is very meaningful to me. For me it is a question asking if the end of something really is the end, or if the beginning of something really is the beginning. These stories I have written never really end. I will never stop remembering them, and people will never stop reading them. End of the beginning, beginning of the end, these stories never end.

As I read this my eyes filled with tears. My son said to me, "You know Mom . . . it's like that story you tell in Godly Play about the church year . . . how for every beginning there is an end and for every ending there is a beginning."

I nodded and said, "Yes. I know. That's why I'm crying."

First, I love that when left alone for the weekend he was able to write such a sensitive and meaningful introduction. Second, and more importantly, it thrilled me then (and does today) how the language from a story he had heard for eleven years in Godly Play about time, welled up in him and spilled out onto the page as he considered all that he had written over the course of the year. We say that the goal of Godly Play is to teach children the art of using religious language to make existential meaning, and there it was happening right in front of me. It seems to work!

I will confess, I hate when people ask me if Godly Play works. This is because I'm not sure what they mean by that. I imagine they are really asking, "Is it easy to do? Do the children like it? Does it really engage them?" No, Godly Play is not easy, and sometimes the children will tell you they don't like it or that they are bored. However, I believe it is what they need, and I have seen that with my own eyes. I also know that my stories alone are not enough. This led me to start a Ph.D. program in psychology so I could learn how to do research on children's spiritual development. I needed to expand my knowledge of how Godly Play works, not just for my son, but for children all over the globe. My research addressed the following questions: Why is it important to nurture a child's spiritual life? If it is important, where are the studies that show how best to do this, especially in the field of religious formation? Since we theorize that Godly Play is one of the best ways to do this, how can we prove it?

Why Is It Important to Nurture a Child's Spiritual Life?

Research indicates that spiritual health is an important resource for the psychological, emotional, and physical well-being of individuals.[2] Studies reveal that spirituality and religion play important roles in coping with stress, specifically in helping military families cope with the stresses related to deployments.[3] The medical field has exhibited an increased interest in the connection between coping with physical or mental illness and spiritual well-being, as shown by a number of studies that indicate a strong correlation between spiritual well-being and strong coping skills for dealing with illness. [4] Wink, Dillon, and Larsen (2005) investigated the long-term relationship between religiousness, spirituality, depression, and physical health. They found that as their sample aged, religiousness and spirituality had a significant buffering effect on depression associated with physical illness, "with highest levels of depression observed in the low-religiousness-poor-physical-health group."[5] Smith (2009) analyzed the positive and negative coping skills of adolescents diagnosed with cancer and found that the patients used positive religious coping strategies more frequently than negative religious coping strategies. For example, patients often spoke of God as someone who would help them get

---

2. C. Allen, *Forming Resilient Children: The Role of Spiritual Formation for Healthy Development* (Downers Grove, IL: InterVarsity Press, 2021).
3. S. Graham, S. Furr, C. Flowers, and M. Burke, "Religion and Spirituality in Coping with Stress," *Counseling and Values,* 46, no. 1 (2001): 2–13. http://www.highbeam.com/doc/1G1-79370592.html.
4. L. M. Nichols and B. Hunt, "The Significance of Spirituality for Individuals with Chronic Illness: Implications for Mental Health Counseling," *Journal of Mental Health Counseling,* 33, no. 1 (2011): 51–66. http://amhca.metapress.com/link.asp?id=025544189523j738.
5. P. Wink, M. Dillon, and B. Larsen, "Religion as Moderator of the Depression-Health Connection: Findings from a Longitudinal Study," *Research on Aging,* 27 (2005): 197. doi: 10.1177/0164027504270483.

through their illness.[6] Zanowski (2009) found that people with strong spiritual coping skills had less severe symptoms of posttraumatic stress.[7] Similarly, Houg's (2009) examination of the role of spirituality in the ongoing recovery process of female sexual abuse survivors found that participants viewed spirituality as the greatest single factor in their recovery.[8]

Studies found that spiritual well-being is connected with healthy behaviors such as diet, exercise, choosing not to engage in risky sexual behaviors, substance abuse, and more.[9] Trauma and grief counselors have long believed it is necessary to address children's spiritual needs, in addition to their psychological and emotional needs, in their efforts to support children in rebuilding after a significant loss.[10] For example, a study on the coping strategies of individuals directly connected to the 9/11 attacks on the World Trade Center in New York suggests strong connections between positive coping skills and spirituality and religious belief.[11] Similarly, studies conducted with survivors of Hurricane Katrina, which impacted New Orleans, Louisiana, and the surrounding areas in September of 2005, found that spirituality and religious belief served as a coping mechanism that allowed them to make meaning and adjust to their new situation.[12]

---

6. J. L. Smith, *Spiritual Coping in Children Diagnosed with Cancer* (doctoral dissertation, George Fox University, 2009). Retrieved from *ProQuest Dissertations and Theses* (document ID: 855629644).

7. S. C. Zanowski, *Spiritual Coping, Distress, and Symptoms of Posttraumatic Stress Disorder Following Traumatic Injury* (doctoral dissertation, Marquette University, 2009). Retrieved from *ProQuest Dissertations and Theses* (document ID: 304919311).

8. B. L. Houg, *The Role of Spirituality in the Ongoing Recovery Process of Female Sexual Abuse Survivors* (doctoral dissertation, University of Minnesota, 2008). Retrieved from *ProQuest Dissertations and Theses* (document ID: 304512145).

9. J. D. Campbell, D. P. Yoon, and B. Johnstone, "Determining Relationships between Physical Health and Spiritual Experience, Religious Practices, and Congregational Support in a Heterogeneous Medical Sample," *Journal of Religion and Health*, 49, no. 1 (2010): 3–17. doi:10.1007/s10943-008-9227-5.

10. R. L. Glick, J. S. Berlin, A. B. Fishkind, and S. Zeller, *Emergency Psychiatry: Principles and Practice* (Philadelphia: Lippincott, Williams, & Wilkins, 2008).

11. J. B. Meisenhelder and J. P. Marcum, "Terrorism, Post-traumatic Stress, Coping Strategies, and Spiritual Outcomes," *Journal of Religion and Health*, 48, no. 1 (2009): 46–57. doi:10.1007/s10943-008-9192-z.

12. J. D. Aten et al., "God Images Following Hurricane Katrina in South Mississippi: An Exploratory Study, *Journal of Psychology and Theology*, 36, no. 4 (2008): 249–257. http://search.proquest.com/docview/223666080?accountid=28180.

Promoting Spiritual Well-Being: Research has Few Answers

Even with strong evidence that spiritual well-being is an important resource for individuals with regard to their overall health, there is very little empirical research on how spiritual well-being can be promoted, even among religious educators. Studies show vague connections between activities planned for children and spirituality, with a complete lack of evidence for any positive, lasting impact on a child's spiritual well-being.[13] In my own research I also found a number of books and articles aimed at educators and parents, most of which contain guidelines or suggestions that are loosely based on research on the way children learn, but do not rise much above the level of good advice.[14]

Measuring the Effectiveness of Godly Play

I set about measuring the effectiveness of Godly Play by designing a quasi-experimental study. The study looked specifically at how Godly Play impacts a child's spiritual well-being.

The theoretical framework for the study was Hay and Nye's theory of children's spirituality.[15] Hay and Nye (2006) proposed that relational consciousness is what allows individuals of all ages to reflect on their spiritual experiences, develop identity and a feeling of worth, and find meaning and purpose in life, which leads in turn to spiritual and emotional well-being. Hay and Nye's research revealed that many individuals repress or discard relational consciousness altogether as they encounter cultural pressures that devalue it. This led them to propose guidelines for adults to follow in an effort to promote spiritual well-being by nurturing relational consciousness in children in both religious and secular settings. Nye (2009), a Godly Play Trainer and leader in the movement, further developed the guidelines, proposing that programs of spiritual formation can promote spiritual well-being when they deliver six conditions important for the nurture of relational

13. M. J. Anthony, ed., *Perspectives on Children's Spiritual Formation: Four Views* (Nashville, TN: Broadman & Holman Publishers, 2006).
14. C. Stonehouse and S. May, *Listening to Children on the Spiritual Journey: Guidance for Those Who Teach and Nurture* (Grand Rapids, MI: Baker Academic, 2010).
15. D. Hay and R. Nye, *The Spirt of the Child,* rev. ed. (London: Jessica Kingsley Publishers, 2006).

consciousness: *space, process, imagination, relationship, intimacy,* and *trust.*[16] Nye had Godly Play in mind as she developed the six conditions. See Appendix E, p. 151, for a complete description of the six conditions and how the Godly Play method delivers them.

The study I conducted was complex, and I will only outline it here in broad strokes. The effect of exposure to Godly Play on spiritual well-being was measured in a sample of children aged five to twelve years who were enrolled and had been enrolled for varying lengths of time (between 12 and 512 weeks, spanning 3 months to 10 years) in a Godly Play program. The dependent variable of spiritual well-being was measured with the *Feeling Good, Living Life* (FGLL) instrument, developed by Fisher (2004) to measure the spiritual well-being of young children aged five to twelve years.[17]

The stability of the effect of exposure to Godly Play after enrollment ended was examined in a sample of children aged ten to twelve years whose exposure to Godly Play ended between 12 to 316 weeks prior (3 months to 6 years). This second part of the study also used the *Feeling Good, Living Life* (FGLL) instrument, developed by Fisher (2004), to measure the spiritual well-being of the sample.

While I did not find a statistically significant relationship between length of time in Godly Play and spiritual well-being, it was very close ($p = 0.22$). The second study did show that the effect remained stable or even increased as time since enrollment increased ($p = 0.06$).

There were many issues that made this study less than perfect, including the inability to accurately measure length of exposure to Godly Play (incomplete attendance figures), and the uncertainty around the fidelity of implementation of the Godly Play method. Even so, the findings were encouraging and follow-up studies that control for these factors would hopefully point to an even greater statistical significance. What is most important is that this study begins to show that Godly Play is not just a method full of well-meaning advice but can be shown to

16. R. Nye, *Children's Spirituality: What It Is and Why It Matters* (London: Church House Publishing, 2009).
17. J. W. Fisher, "Feeling Good, Living Life: A Spiritual Health Measure for Young Children," *Journal of Beliefs and Values*, 25, no. 3 (2004): 307-315. doi: 10.1080/1361767042000306121.

effectively nurture a child's spiritual life. More compelling than any statistic, however, are the voices of the children who experienced Godly Play not just as very young children, but all the way through early, middle, and late childhood. It is time to hear from them.

The Voices of the Children

In the surveys of churches using Godly Play with children in middle and late childhood mentioned throughout this book, I asked if they would help me get in touch with some of the "graduates" of those programs; young adults who had experienced the full breadth of the spiral curriculum. I received a number of contacts and was able to conduct several interviews over Zoom. With the help of Zoom's transcribing tool, you will hear directly from each one about what they remember about Godly Play, and how it continues to impact them as young adults.

Each interviewee was asked roughly the same questions, with some variations based on their responses: What did you like best about Godly Play when you were a little child? What did you like about Godly Play when you got older? What do you remember most about all your time in Godly Play? What was your favorite story when you were little? What is your favorite story now? Was there any time when Godly Play was challenging or frustrating for you? As you think back on our years in Godly Play, what part seems most important?

Mitchell

Mitchell is a seventeen-year-old who attended Godly Play from ages three to thirteen. His father volunteered as a door person in the Godly Play program at his church, so he was in attendance on a very regular basis. In his interview he mentioned loving the stories, especially anything in the desert box, and also work time. But what really stands out in Mitchell's interview is the importance of the community that was formed for him in Godly Play. He said,

> When I was young, I really liked listening to stories and then afterwards, you'd have time to color. But as I grew older, I still enjoyed the stories, but I also enjoyed being able to talk to other people and make new friends. The most important part for me was probably that—the relationships. We really bonded over those stories.

Mitchell attended Godly Play with the same group of children for eleven years. That alone contributed to his feeling of closeness to that group. But equally important is the way the Godly Play method supports the relationships he described; it creates a sense of mutual respect and safety. The storytellers are trained to help build the kind of trust and mutual respect that grew into important friendships, not just between the children, but between the children and the adult mentors as well. Mitchell spoke in his interview about how important those mentors still are to him now that he is a junior in high school. He looks forward to seeing them at church and finds time to connect every week.

Mitchell went on to talk about Godly Play, and by extension the entire church, as "a place of safety" for him. He said he didn't realize it wasn't something everyone had; that it was unique, saying, "Why would they do something else?" He said he would sometimes think about it during the week and think how great it would be to be back with those friends in the Godly Play Room. Mitchell mentioned that they are still all good friends, and he loves to go to church and see them, serve with them as an acolyte and on the tech team, and visit after church.

Sarah

Sarah is Mitchell's sister. She is a little bit younger, so asked if she could be interviewed with him. She just moved out of Godly Play (she is in the ninth grade). For Sarah the relationships were also very important. She also talked about specific stories. She said she especially liked the "getting ready times" like Advent and Lent. She liked that we revisited the stories regularly and said that she felt it gave them a chance to "understand and comprehend it more, like what it really means to you now that you are older." She said that her favorite story is the story of Creation because it always caused her to stop and think about all that God has given us. Sarah didn't really want to stop going to Godly Play, so now that she is in high school, she is serving as a door person.

Alexander

Alexander is a senior in high school. He did Godly Play from ages three to thirteen. Like Mitchell's experience above, Alexander's circle remained stable all throughout his years in Godly Play. Furthermore, this group had much the same group of mentors throughout their years in Godly Play. All of this contributed to the building of strong relationships and made the room feel like a safe place to be themselves and explore the meaning of the stories through wonder. When we asked Alexander what part he liked best as a child, he quickly answered the response time. He remembered loving having the open-ended time to draw. But he said that as he got older, he came to value the stories too. He said,

> The stories were presented in a more understandable way, you can engage with it more, there were little pieces you can move around, which was fun. It wasn't, you know, silence and you just listen to one person. You can talk and have a conversation, and you could ask questions. It was nice getting to talk to everyone, make some friends, and have a bit of choice time where you can choose to do something creative or that you'd like to do. I remember the stories being really interesting. I actually enjoyed the challenge, when I got older, of looking into some of the deeper meanings that they offered.

When asked what was the most important part of Godly Play, Alexander spoke about both the stories and the community. He said,

> It (Godly Play) was how I learned about the Bible and about how church works. When I was young, I could not understand anything they talked about in the main service, but I could understand what was being talked about in Godly Play. And that allowed me to make connections, when I *was* able to understand what was going on in the main church, and I could relate it back to my years in Godly Play. But also remember all the fun we had, the jokes and laughter that my classmates and I had. We still joke about it sometimes today.

As with Mitchell, the kind of community that was formed for Alexander in Godly Play was no accident. The storytellers are trained not only to tell creative Bible stories, but to create a safe place for the community of children to wonder and work together to make meaning with the stories. That creates deep bonds of respect and affection that, in Alexander's case, continue to be an important part of his spiritual and religious life.

Matthew

Matthew is a senior in high school who grew up in Godly Play as well. His mother is a Godly Play Trainer, so everywhere they went she built a Godly Play Room and he was part of those circles. In many ways it became part of the fabric of their family life. All of them "spoke Godly Play" both in the circles at church and at home. He laughed as he talked about how the language creeps into their family life, saying, "My sister and I will tease my mother about it, saying lines from the stories as we eat dinner, etcetera." When Matthew was asked what he liked most about Godly Play he said,

> I would say when I was very young, it was the visual part. I've always been someone who was a very visual learner. I think moving forward, and growing older, what became more important for me was just my curiosity with the stories themselves. You know, as you get older, you start to notice some of the themes of these stories and some of the deeper meanings and messages that you just don't get on a surface level as a little kid.

Matthew talked about valuing the consistency of Godly Play in his life. He loved that the room didn't change, and he could see all that was there. He described the time they moved to a new place, and finding another Godly Play Room there. He was so happy to see all of it in that new place. Matthew said that the Exodus story was probably his favorite story.. He said that it just seemed to be sort of timeless.

> I always liked the messaging behind it . . . of God doing what was necessary to lead his people, to the promised land, and the symbolism of, of Moses being a leader . . . fulfilling his duties and just a small component of him not being able to follow them into the promised land.

Matthew went on to say,

> I think the most important part of Godly Play for me was the foundation that it gave me for the stories that are in the Bible. I think it produced an incredibly important foundation for me as a young religious kid. Like it gave me a purpose for being at Church each week.

Throughout Matthew's interview I could hear him connecting the stories he learned in Godly Play to his own life and to the things he was studying at school.

He reflected many times on how much he appreciated the wondering as well, describing it as an opportunity to really think about the stories and what they meant to him then, but also now that he is older. He laughed and talked about how he makes fun of wondering from time to time with his mother, but that it is probably the thing that sticks with him the most as he thinks about the stories now.

Jonathan

Jonathan, a twenty-year-old college student, had Godly Play from ages three to thirteen (or so). Like some of the others interviewed, his mother is a Godly Play Trainer, so it was not just something he experienced on Sunday mornings; it was woven into his family life as well. The story materials would often be at home as his mother practiced them, and the books were always around the house. Jonathan said that as a young child he loved "playing with the stuff." As he got older, he also really enjoyed the art response materials in the room.

Jonathan valued the consistency of the program, mentioning specifically how the room would not change dramatically as he moved through the program. He said, "It meant that even though the teachers and students might be a little different, everything would be there. It meant there was less to figure out."

Jonathan's favorite story was the Parable of the Mustard Seed. When asked why, he talked about the specifics of the story and how much he loved watching the tree grow from the tiny seed. He could not find the words to describe why he liked it so much, but it led him to reflect on how he admired the way stories were told in Godly Play generally, and that he aspires to be that kind of storyteller now, finding important connections to it even in his current internship. Jonathan also mentioned loving the lesson on the church year found in Volume 2 of the *The Complete Guide to Godly Play*. He said he continues to think about time in that way, as a kind of circle.

Throughout Jonathan's interview I heard him reflecting on how the experience of Godly Play continues to be important now. He spoke often of how the process of Godly Play informs how he approaches things now. He described it as an opportunity to think seriously about the stories and what they meant "theologically."

James

James, a thirty-year-old, attended Godly Play from ages six to twelve both in Sunday school and at the Episcopal school he attended. He also remembered Godly Play being a part of his summer camp experience and as part of "Journey to Adulthood," a program for older youth. When asked what he remembers most about it, he spoke of the stories and the art response time. He really values how Godly Play connected his creative self with his spiritual self. However, what seemed most important to James was the way Godly Play encouraged him and his peers to ask questions. He said,

> As I got older there was definitely more cerebral engagement. It wasn't just about understanding the stories at that point, but was about looking for analogies . . . or wondering if this story or that one could be an analogy for a problem or an issue I'm having, you know, in my world, my life, whatever. And then, as a much older adult, that practice enables me to engage with people of all sorts in a thoughtful way.

James spoke powerfully about how Godly Play supported him when he first started questioning his faith (around aged ten or eleven) and kept him engaged in the life of the church. He said that without Godly Play, he thinks he would have had a crisis of faith and walked away from the church. Godly Play allowed him to see the value in the community and stories, even if he wasn't sure what he really believed. He felt comfortable asking the hard questions, and comfortable just living with those questions.

James's favorite story was the story of the Great Family. He said that as a young person he enjoyed the desert box, and specifically talked about how they kept building altars in the places where God was. As he grew older, he saw it more as about learning to let go of the things that are unimportant. He reflected on this saying that change is never easy and often involves some hardship. He said that those kinds of things cause you to think deeply about what is truly important; help you to let go of the stuff that is not, "or to let go of some of the stuff that is essential and being okay."

Throughout James's interview he pulled on the language of the stories to try and describe what he was thinking. He often did this subconsciously, and at other times more explicitly. It was clear that the language is very much a part of his daily life, and that it continues to help him "make meaning" about his life, his faith, really everything, as a young adult.

Mary

Mary is a twenty-two-year-old who attended Godly Play for about six years as a child. Like many of the others interviewed she loved the visual aspect of Godly Play and the wondering. Mary spoke movingly about how as a young child, the teachers in the room made her feel safe, and took her seriously. She said,

> I liked building a relationship with whoever was teaching, whoever was in the classroom with us . . . sitting down and talking and having everything you say be taken seriously. The teacher took the time to really listen to everyone in the room. That felt good.

As Mary grew older she really came to value the wondering questions and the whole process of wondering. She said,

> That kind of questioning and making sure that your faith has room for doubt was really important. I heard a lot of my friends that attended different churches or different religions complaining about church. They said there wasn't really any room to ask questions, because everyone around them seemed to just believe it all. I think if you have so much doubt about what you are learning, your faith isn't going to get stronger . . . unless you resolve it, or discuss it openly like we did in Godly Play.

Mary ended by saying that she would strongly recommend Godly Play to others with a bit of a caveat. She said,

> Godly Play will be good for you if you're interested in providing an education of faith rather than just Bible classes. Godly Play is not just Bible classes, where you are just given scripture and you extract information from it. Godly Play really brings you into the story and gives you the opportunity to ask why.

Danny

Danny is a twenty-year-old who attended Godly Play from ages three to thirteen or fourteen. She said that as a young child her family ended up going to a specific church because of Godly Play. The first time they visited she went to a session and asked afterwards, "Can we go to church tomorrow?" The whole family got very involved at the church, and her mother became a storyteller. As a young child Danny loved the stories and valued the way they were presented. She said,

> I think the stories were very engaging and understandable. And I didn't feel like I was being led in a certain direction. You were really allowed to have your own thoughts and feelings about the story. I never ever felt personally that I could say something wrong.

Having her mother as a storyteller was never a problem for Danny. She said,

> I didn't ever really feel like we had, you know, a mother-daughter relationship during the class because it was like we're all listening to the stories. My mother was not an expert or anything, just another person listening to the story.

That feeling is intentionally part of a Godly Play session. The storyteller may be presenting the story or lesson, but the story is placed on the floor, in the middle of the circle, and the storyteller is sitting on the same level as the children. All of this helps to facilitate the feeling that everyone is approaching the story on equal footing. Danny said this remained a part of her experience as she got older. She said that when she and her friends aged out of the program, they asked her mother to come to their gatherings and share more of the stories. They did not want to stop wondering about the stories together.

Danny's favorite stories were the ones about Moses interacting with God on Mt. Sinai. She loved the visuals of the mountain, and the way the storyteller moved the figure for Moses into the cloud of smoke that covered the mountain. She found the way the storyteller spoke of Moses and God's encounter very compelling and continues to think about that today. She said,

> I remember something that comes up a lot in Godly Play. They talk about how the people come so close to God and God comes so close to them. That's just something I remember over and over, and I think about often when describing someone who is divinely inspired and their relationship with God. I see that Godly Play has influenced me immensely in the way of thinking about relationships with God. The relationship is not about God speaking to you, and is more about a connection . . . someone coming so close to God and God

comes so close that they could talk and experience each other. More of a two-way street.

Danny really valued the ability to think about the stories independently. She said,

I would say that what was most important to me was the ability for me to have my own relationship with the stories. I was never once given the option of believing the story or not, per se. I was never really told how to think about the story. The story was just there. And I could interact with it, how I wanted. And I could draw my own conclusions from the story. And that has been something that has carried me through in my adult life.

John

John, a twenty-six-year-old, attended Godly Play from ages three to thirteen. His mother was often the storyteller, so he often spoke of her during the interview. When he was a sophomore in college, he attended a Godly Play Core Training and helped get Godly Play going at the church near his college. When asked what part he liked best as a child, John mentioned the "tactile elements" of Godly Play. He said,

I really enjoyed the visual aspect of it. I think it really made stories more approachable, and then it gave me a foundation, like an imagery foundation as I got older, to kind of build off my understanding of the stories. And I really enjoyed sitting on the floor. I think that—especially being the loud, rambunctious, ADHD kid that I was—I think that it helped me center my attention . . . kept me from feeling jittery . . . gave me an environment where I could really focus.

As an older child John said he liked the wondering the best. He spoke of watching other children struggle with the openness of the wondering, but that for him it was his favorite part. He said,

I really enjoyed feeling like anything that I had to say was validated and was valid and would lead to other conversational points with my peers, leading into larger conversations after that. And I just really enjoyed the inwardly focused aspect of reflection that I don't think I was really finding anywhere else, certainly not at that point in my life.

When John was asked how Godly Play changed as he got older, he continued to talk about the wondering, reflecting that it got much more "substantial" when he was older. He mentioned feeling as if wondering was really central to his experience when he got older, even more important than the actual story that was told.

John also talked about loving the desert stories, and working with the desert during response time. But his favorite story was the Good Shepherd. He said,

> That one has always stuck with me. It's always right there on the surface for me to dip back into. It was also the first story that I learned when I started telling stories myself. But even when I was young, it was always something that I felt like I was able to really dig into and reflect on. I know I said wondering was more substantial when I got older, but that's not the case for that story. It was something that I really could see a lot of my own experience in, especially with, like, my struggles with ADHD. And just thinking about the bad places in my life, like high school and relationships, and social interactions and moments where I may feel, you know, uncomfortable or scared . . . that like God was there . . . meeting us where we are in the good places in the bad places and in the in-between ones. It helped me see God in my life.

When asked how he thinks about the story now, he spoke of the ordinary shepherd in the parable, saying,

> In this day and age there are endless numbers of ordinary shepherds that people are following in their lives. But in the face of true adversity those ordinary shepherds flee. Whether we accept God or not, God is always there. But in those difficult moments, those kind of false ideas of a shepherd aren't there. You're not looking in the right direction for safety, or inspiration or identity, or fulfillment, or meaning. You know, like your work or career could be like an ordinary shepherd, or a relationship could be an ordinary shepherd. That's not to say that these are bad things, but those things won't be there for you when you really need them . . . like the Good Shepherd.

John did name some challenges. He said that at times the *wondering* (his favorite part) was hard, as he struggled to make sense of all that he was feeling. It wasn't that Godly Play was bad, but that he was getting input from so many places that it felt challenging to get at all the layers of meaning in a story or lesson. At the same time, he talked about how powerful it was to be allowed to wonder, and then in turn watching the children in the circle he started at college begin to wonder as well. He said that whenever he talks to his peers about Godly Play he always focuses on the wondering. He mentions that they are always surprised to hear about it since they have this idea in their heads that Sunday school was just a bunch of adults telling children how to think and feel about God. John ended by saying that it (wondering) is just astounding . . . and that it just makes him happy to think of it happening in circles all over the world.

Throughout John's interview we can hear him using the language of Godly Play in meaningful ways. It seems as if the stories live deep inside of him and are as much a part of him as his love of swimming and boating. He uses the language to reflect deeply on his own life struggles—struggles to fit in as a child with learning issues, struggles to find a meaningful career, relationship struggles, and more. You can hear how deeply comforting the images are for him, and how they sustain him through the difficult things. God seems also to be real for him, someone who is with him in "the good, the bad, and in-between times." It is hard to miss the importance of the practice of wondering was for him as a child, and how that continues to animate his life today. He loved it as a child, but it became very important when he grew older. So often churches stop using Godly Play with children after about age eight, and so they will miss the opportunity for the kind of substantial wondering and deep reflection John describes. What's more, it is clear that John (and all the young adults we interviewed) is continuing to wonder about the stories as an adult, and that is exactly how the spiral of Godly Play is meant to function; as children practice the art of making meaning with these stories in circles with trained Godly Play mentors, they are equipped to continue finding new insights throughout their lives.

Conclusion

I often hear people on social media saying that their children are "over Godly Play"; that they need something new. My hope is that this book will be something those people turn to when they don't know what else to do; that it will help them find both practical tools and inspiration to keep going. Does Godly Play work? It seems like it. But what is more important is that Godly Play seems to be what children need. They need the space it provides to grow spiritually. Godly Play does not turn children into a particular sort of Christian. While you can hear themes in the responses of those interviews (they loved the stories, the wondering, and so on), each one is a thoughtful young adult who is continuing to use the language and process they learned in Godly Play to make meaning.

As I conclude, I want to share one more story about my son. This happened when he was in the ninth grade, a freshman in high school. One Friday in the early fall, a young girl decided to end her life by walking in front of a commuter train—the train that runs on a track right behind the high school. It happened during school hours. The faculty and staff worked hard to shield the students in the school from the worst of it, moving them away from classrooms that overlooked the train tracks and keeping them in the building until the accident was cleared away. But they all knew what had happened. Eventually the students were released from school.

My son called me to tell me what had happened and to ask for a ride home. As it turned out I was sick in bed. I had a high fever and could not get out of bed to get him. He had to walk home. When he arrived, he came up to my bedroom and sat and talked for a bit. I wasn't much help, so eventually he disappeared into his room. He was there for a long time. He loves music and I heard him playing the Brahm's *Requiem*, a piece he had been studying with his teacher. He followed along with the score and let the rich music fill his soul.

The next day when I finally emerged from my bed I went into his room. He was busy with something and I went in to pick things up a bit. On his bed I found several drawings he had done while listening to the music. One caught my eye. It was a cross that was light on one side, and then became gradually darker. There was what looked like chaos on the dark side of the cross. But on the light side he had carefully written the words of the Lord's Prayer (see Appendix F, p. 159). I never asked him about it. I felt like it was something private that he probably didn't mean for me to see. But I saw in the drawing echoes of the story we tell in Godly Play called "the Mystery of Easter" (*The Complete Guide to Godly Play*, Volume 4, Lesson 1). Those of you who are experienced with Godly Play will remember that in that presentation the storyteller pulls wooden pieces of all different shapes and sizes from a purple bag (the liturgical color for Lent). The children watch as the pieces are pushed together to form a purple cross. But then the storyteller turns the pieces over to reveal a white cross (the liturgical color for Easter). The sadness and seriousness of Lent come together with the happiness of Easter to make joy. Joy is different from happiness. There is always some struggle involved in joy.

My son was struggling to understand why anyone would end their life, and in such a horrible way. The Easter story was helping in some way, but it would likely be the kind of thing he would keep working on for his whole life. Had I been well, I might have tried to talk with him more. The truth of the matter is that he knew what to do. He reached into his tool box and got busy making sense of it. He didn't really need my help after all.

Jerome Berryman writes that,

> The goal of Godly Play is for children to move through the spiral curriculum during early, middle and late childhood in such a way that they will enter adolescence with an inner working model of the classical Christian language system to root them deeply in the Tradition and at the same time allow them to be open to the future.

This does not happen if children stop doing Godly Play after just three or four years. They need the full breadth of the spiral, moving through early, middle, and late childhood, to internalize both the language and the process of using it to make meaning.

I have served at the same church as co-rector (with my spouse) for over twenty years. I have seen many children work their way through the entire spiral. We have a tradition that as they finish the eighth grade, we gather them at the front of the church to pray for them as a community. Each one receives an "at-home" version of the Parable of the Good Shepherd. The inscription inside the cover of the box reads:

> *This parable is given to you with thanksgiving for our years of wondering together in Godly Play. Now you can tell the stories! Here is one to get your started. With love from all your Godly Play mentors at All Saints' Church in Belmont, Massachusetts.*

After I pray for them, I always say, "I hope you will carry this with you wherever you go . . . because you never know when you might need a parable." They smile and nod. They know exactly what I mean.

Some of the children at All Saints' in Belmont, Massachusetts, receiving their at-home version of the Parable of the Good Shepherd.

There is a wonderful picture book by Barry Lopez called *Crow and Weasel*.[18] It is the story of a crow and a weasel who go on a great journey. At some point they stop to rest at the home of an old badger. They spend the evening enjoying good food and sharing stories of their journey. The badger, being old and wise, is a wonderful listener. He also coaches them as they tell the story, asking for more feeling or details as they go. The next morning, as he wishes them farewell, he says,

> I would ask you to remember only this one thing: The stories people tell have a way of taking care of them. If stories come to you, care for them. And learn to give them away where they are needed. Sometimes a person needs a story more than food to stay alive. That is why we put these stories in each other's memory. This is how people care for themselves.

18. B. Lopez, *Crow and Weasel* (San Francisco: Northpoint Press, 1990).

Children in middle and late childhood do not stop needing the stories. I am hopeful that more than anything else I have written, the voices of the children will inspire you to keep going, because "Sometimes a person needs a story more than food to stay alive."

Appendix A

Maps of the Godly Play Room

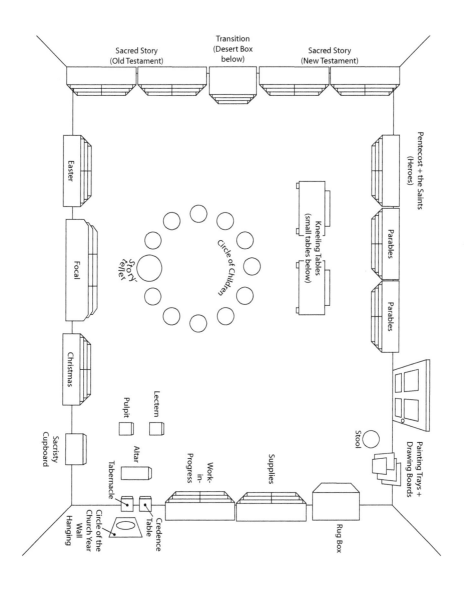

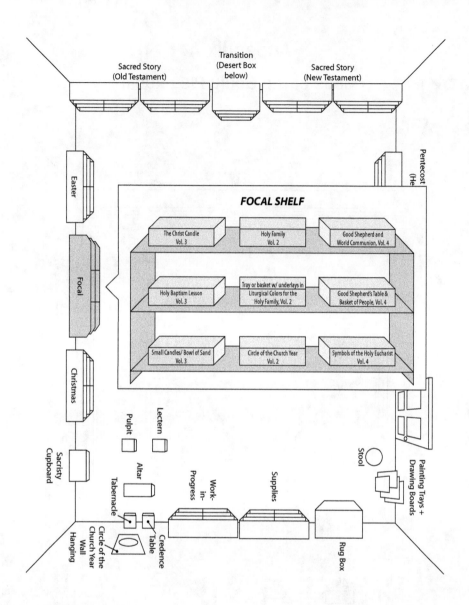

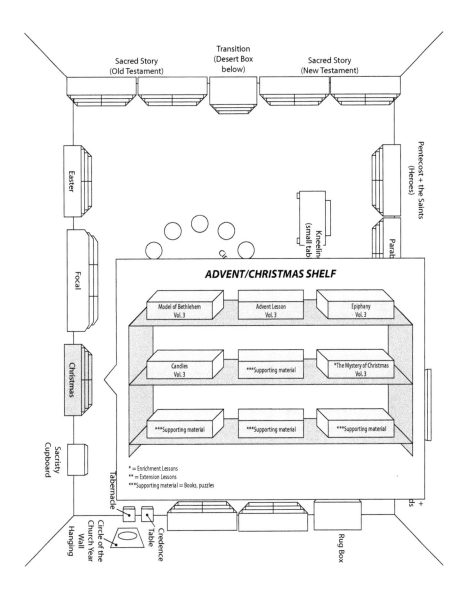

Transition
(Desert Box below)

Sacred Story
(Old Testament)

Sacred Story
(New Testament)

Pentecost + the Saints
(Heroes)

Easter

Focal

Kneeling
(small table)

Parab

Circle

Christmas

ADVENT/CHRISTMAS SHELF

Model of Bethlehem Vol. 3	Advent Lesson Vol. 3	Epiphany Vol. 3
Candles Vol. 3	***Supporting material	*The Mystery of Christmas Vol. 3
***Supporting material	***Supporting material	***Supporting material

* = Enrichment Lessons
** = Extension Lessons
***Supporting material = Books, puzzles

Sacristy Cupboard

Tabernacle

Circle of the Church Year Wall Hanging

Credence Table

Rug Box

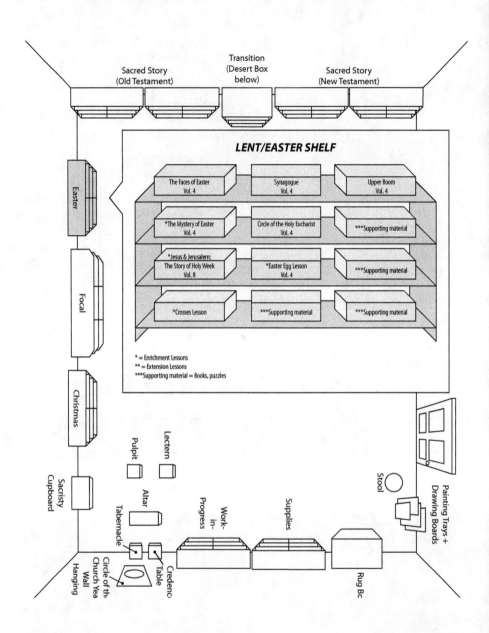

LENT/EASTER SHELF

The Faces of Easter Vol. 4	Synagogue Vol. 4	Upper Room Vol. 4
*The Mystery of Easter Vol. 4	Circle of the Holy Eucharist Vol. 4	***Supporting material
*Jesus & Jerusalem: The Story of Holy Week Vol. 8	*Easter Egg Lesson Vol. 4	***Supporting material
*Crosses Lesson	***Supporting material	***Supporting material

* = Enrichment Lessons
** = Extension Lessons
***Supporting material = Books, puzzles

Sacred Story (Old Testament)

Transition (Desert Box below)

Sacred Story (New Testament)

Easter

Focal

Christmas

Sacristy Cupboard

Pulpit

Lectern

Altar

Tabernacle

Work-in-Progress

Supplies

Stool

Painting Trays + Drawing Boards

Circle of th Church Yea Wall Hanging

Credenc Table

Rug Bc

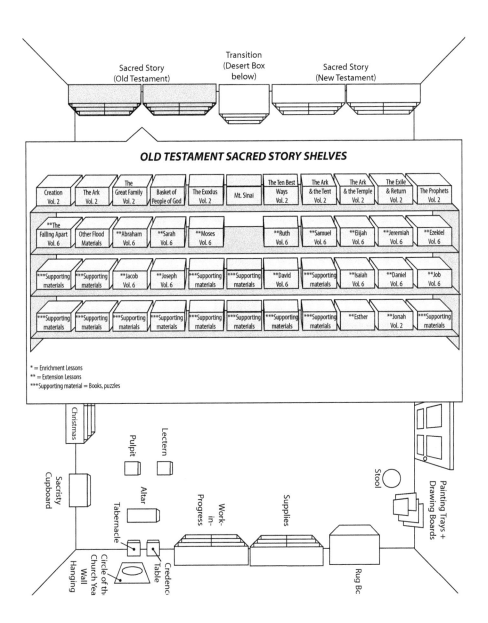

OLD TESTAMENT SACRED STORY SHELVES

Creation Vol. 2	The Ark Vol. 2	The Great Family Vol. 2	Basket of People of God	The Exodus Vol. 2	Mt. Sinai	The Ten Best Ways Vol. 2	The Ark & the Tent Vol. 2	The Ark & the Temple Vol. 2	The Exile & Return Vol. 2	The Prophets Vol. 2	
**The Falling Apart Vol. 6	Other Flood Materials	**Abraham Vol. 6	**Sarah Vol. 6	**Moses Vol. 6		**Ruth Vol. 6	**Samuel Vol. 6	**Elijah Vol. 6	**Jeremiah Vol. 6	**Ezekiel Vol. 6	
***Supporting materials	***Supporting materials	**Jacob Vol. 6	**Joseph Vol. 6	***Supporting materials	***Supporting materials	**David Vol. 6	***Supporting materials	**Isaiah Vol. 6	**Daniel Vol. 6	**Job Vol. 6	
***Supporting materials	***Supporting materials	***Supporting materials	***Supporting materials	***Supporting materials	***Supporting materials	***Supporting materials	***Supporting materials	**Esther	**Jonah Vol. 2	***Supporting materials	

* = Enrichment Lessons
** = Extension Lessons
***Supporting material = Books, puzzles

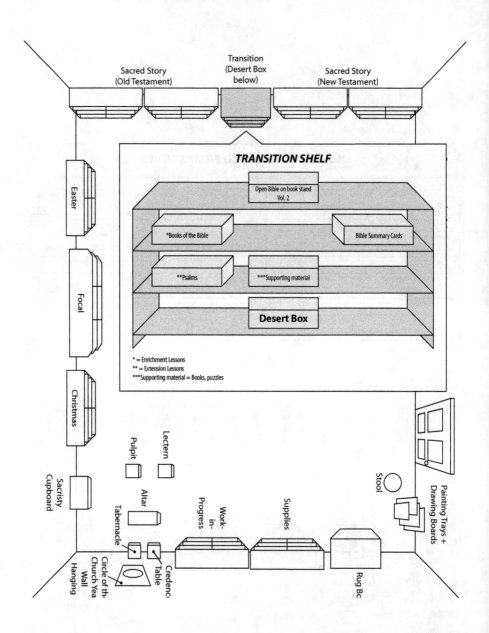

Appendix A

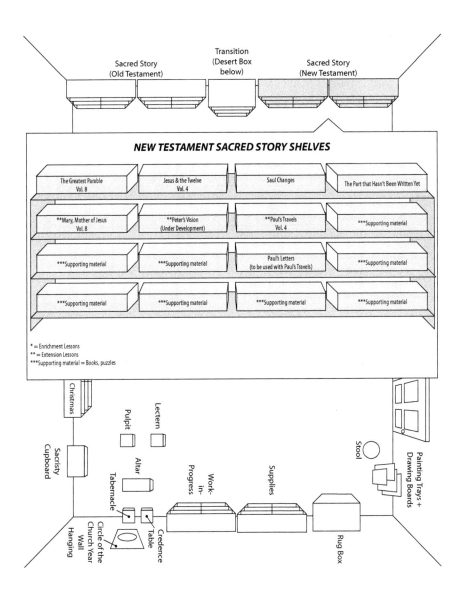

Sacred Story (Old Testament)

Transition (Desert Box below)

Sacred Story (New Testament)

NEW TESTAMENT SACRED STORY SHELVES

| The Greatest Parable Vol. 8 | Jesus & the Twelve Vol. 4 | Saul Changes | The Part that Hasn't Been Written Yet |

| **Mary, Mother of Jesus Vol. 8 | **Peter's Vision (Under Development) | **Paul's Travels Vol. 4 | ***Supporting material |

| ***Supporting material | ***Supporting material | Paul's Letters (to be used with Paul's Travels) | ***Supporting material |

| ***Supporting material | ***Supporting material | ***Supporting material | ***Supporting material |

* = Enrichment Lessons
** = Extension Lessons
***Supporting material = Books, puzzles

Christmas

Sacristy Cupboard

Pulpit

Lectern

Altar

Tabernacle

Work-in-Progress

Supplies

Stool

Painting Trays + Drawing Boards

Circle of the Church Year Wall Hanging

Credence Table

Rug Box

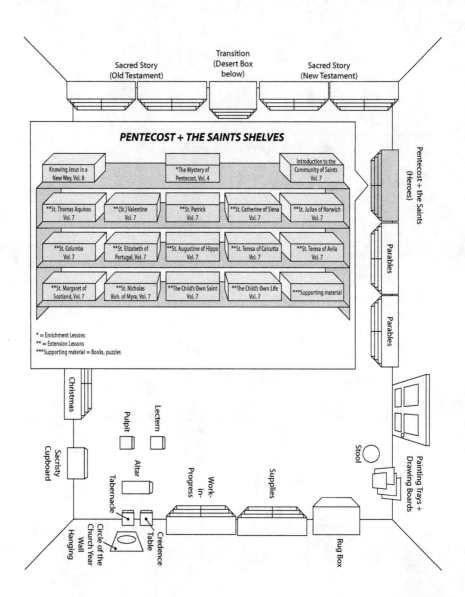

Sacred Story (Old Testament)

Transition (Desert Box below)

Sacred Story (New Testament)

PENTECOST + THE SAINTS SHELVES

Knowing Jesus in a New Way, Vol. 8

*The Mystery of Pentecost, Vol. 4

Introduction to the Community of Saints Vol. 7

**St. Thomas Aquinas Vol. 7

**(St.) Valentine Vol. 7

**St. Patrick Vol. 7

**St. Catherine of Siena Vol. 7

**St. Julian of Norwich Vol. 7

**St. Columba Vol. 7

**St. Elizabeth of Portugal, Vol. 7

**St. Augustine of Hippo Vol. 7

**St. Teresa of Calcutta Vol. 7

**St. Teresa of Avila Vol. 7

**St. Margaret of Scotland, Vol. 7

**St. Nicholas Bish. of Myra, Vol. 7

**The Child's Own Saint Vol. 7

**The Child's Own Life Vol. 7

***Supporting material

* = Enrichment Lessons
** = Extension Lessons
***Supporting material = Books, puzzles

Pentecost + the Saints (Heroes)

Parables

Parables

Christmas

Sacristy Cupboard

Pulpit

Lectern

Altar

Tabernacle

Work-in-Progress

Supplies

Stool

Painting Trays + Drawing Boards

Circle of the Church Year Wall Hanging

Credence Table

Rug Box

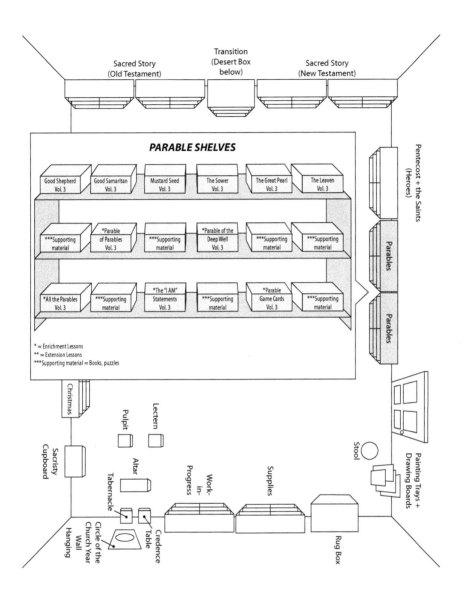

Appendix B
Chart of the Spiral Curriculum

Core Presentations (Ages 3–6, 6–9, 9–12)	Extensions (Ages 6–9, 9–12)	Enrichments (Ages 6–9, 9–12)	Synthesis (Ages 9–12)
Sacred Story			
The Holy Family, v. 1	Mary, v. 8		The Sacred Story Synthesis, v. 2 ↓
The Holy Bible, v. 2	Books of the Bible, v. 2		
	Psalms, v. 6		
Creation, v. 2	The Falling Apart, v. 6		
The Ark & the Flood, v. 2			
The Great Family, v. 2	Abraham, v. 6		
	Sarah, v. 6		
	Jacob, v. 6		
	Joseph, v. 6		
The Exodus, v. 2	Moses, v. 6		
The Ten Best Ways, v. 2			
The Ark & the Tent, v. 2	Ruth, v. 6		
	Samuel, v. 6		
The Ark & the Temple, v. 2	David, v. 6		
The Exile & Return, v. 2	Esther, v. 6		
The Prophets, v. 2	Elijah, v. 6		
	Isaiah, v. 6		
	Jeremiah, v. 6		
	Ezekiel, v. 6		
	Jonah, v. 6		
	Daniel, v. 6		
	Job, v. 6		
The Greatest Parable, v. 8			
Saul Changes, v. 2	Paul's Travels & Letters, v. 2		

Jesus & the Twelve, v. 4			
Liturgical Action			
Circle of the Church Year, v. 2			Liturgical Synthesis, v. 8 ↓
Advent I-IV & Christmas, v. 3			
Epiphany, v. 3			
Holy Baptism, v. 3			
Faces of Easter, v. 4		The Mystery of Easter, v. 4	
		Jesus & Jerusalem, v. 8	
		The Legend of the Easter Egg, v. 4	
Knowing Jesus in a New Way, v. 8	The Mystery of Pentecost, v. 4		
Good Shepherd & World Communion, v. 4			
Synagogue & the Upper Room, v. 4			
Circle of the Holy Eucharist, v. 4		Symbols of the Holy Eucharist, v. 4	
Parables			
Good Shepherd, v. 3		The Deep Well, v. 3	Parable Synthesis, v. 8 ↓
Great Pearl, v. 3		Parable of Parables, v. 3	
Sower, v. 3			
Leaven, v. 3			
Mustard Seed, v. 3			
Good Samaritan, v. 3			
Contemplative Silence			
Making Silence, v. 3			

After the Biblical Era			
The Part That Hasn't Been Written Yet, v. 4		The Crosses, v. 4	
The Church, v. 8			
Intro. to the Communion of Saints, v. 7	Extended Intro. to the Communion of Saints, v. 7		
	Thomas Aquinas, v. 7		
	Valentine, v. 7		
	Patrick, v. 7		
	Catherine of Siena, v. 7		
	Julian of Norwich, v. 7		
	Columba, v. 7		
	Elizabeth of Portugal, v. 7		
	Augustine of Hippo, v. 7		
	Mother Teresa of Calcutta, v. 7		
	Teresa of Avila, v. 7		
	Margaret of Scotland, v. 7		
	Nicholas, Bishop of Myra, v. 7		
	The Story of the Child's Own Saint, v. 7		
	The Story of the Child's Own life, v.7		
People of Color Who Inspire Series	The Rev. Dr. Martin Luther King Jr.		
	Bishop Barbara Harris		
	Congressman John Lewis		
	Harriet Tubman		

For a full outline of Godly Play's spiral curriculum, see the appendix of *The Complete Guide to Godly Play*, Vol. 2, Revised and Expanded.

Appendix C
Sample Story Schedules

Story Schedule Year 1

Sunday	Pre-school–K	Grades 1–3	Grades 4–8
Sept. 15	Circle of the Church Year Vol. 2	Circle of the Church Year Vol. 2	Circle of the Church Year Vol. 2
Sept. 22	The Holy Bible Vol. 2	The Books of the Bible Vol. 2	The Books of the Bible Vol. 2
Sept. 29	The Holy Family Vol. 2	Creation Vol. 2	The Falling Apart Vol. 6
Oct. 6	Creation Vol. 2	The Great Family Vol. 2	Sarah Vol. 6
Oct. 13 Columbus Day w/end	The Ark & the Flood Vol. 2	Moses Vol. 6	Jacob Vol. 6
Oct. 20	The Parable of the Good Shepherd	The Parable of the Good Shepherd	The Parable of the Good Shepherd
Oct. 27	The Great Family Vol. 2	The Ark & the Tent Vol. 2	Joseph Vol. 6
Nov. 3 All Saints' Sunday	Baptism Vol. 3	Baptism Vol. 3	Baptism Vol. 3
Nov. 10	The Exodus Vol. 2	Ruth Vol. 6	Ten Best Ways Vol. 2
Nov. 17	The Parable of the Mustard Seed Vol. 3	Samuel Vol. 6	The Exile & Return Vol. 2
Nov. 24	The Ark & the Tent Vol. 2	The Prophets Vol. 2	Esther Vol. 6
Dec. 1 Thanksgiving w/ end	Combined Class Change Colors—Advent 1 Vol. 3	Combined Class Change Colors—Advent 1 Vol. 3	Combined Class Change Colors—Advent 1 Vol. 3
Dec. 8	Advent 1–2 Vol. 3	Advent 1–2 Vol. 3	Mary Vol. 8
Dec. 15	No class Pageant Sunday	No class Pageant Sunday	No class Pageant Sunday
Dec. 22	Advent 1–4 + peek at Xmas Vol. 3	Advent 1–4 + peek at Xmas Vol. 3	Advent 1–4 + peek at Xmas Vol. 3

Sunday	Pre-school–K	Grades 1–3	Grades 4–8
Dec. 29	Combined Class The Mystery of Christmas Vol. 3	Combined Class The Mystery of Christmas Vol. 3	Combined Class The Mystery of Christmas Vol. 3
Jan. 5	Epiphany Vol. 3	Epiphany Vol. 3	Epiphany Vol. 3
Jan. 12	Intro. to Saints Vol. 7	Expanded Intro. to Saints Vol. 7	Expanded Intro. to Saints Vol. 7
Jan. 19 *MLK w/end*	*Combined Class* MLK Jr. People of Color Who Inspire series	*Combined Class* MLK Jr. People of Color Who Inspire series	*Combined Class* MLK Jr. People of Color Who Inspire series
Jan. 26	The Ark & the Temple Vol. 2	Elijah Vol. 6	Ezekiel Vol. 6
Feb. 2	The Exile & Return Vol. 2	The Leaven Vol. 3	The Leaven & Sower Side by Side Vol. 3
Feb. 9	The Parable of the Sower Vol. 3	Jeremiah Vol. 6	The Mustard Seed & Pearl Side by Side Vol. 3
Feb. 16 *Public School Vacation*	*Combined Class* The Good Samaritan Vol. 3	*Combined Class* The Good Samaritan Vol. 3	*Combined Class* The Good Samaritan Vol. 3
Feb. 23 *Public School Vacation*	*Combined Class* The Parable of Parables Vol. 3	*Combined Class* The Parable of Parables Vol. 3	*Combined Class* The Parable of Parables Vol. 3
March 2	The Pearl Vol. 3	St. Patrick Vol. 7	The Parable Games Vol. 3
March 9 *First Sunday in Lent*	Change Colors & the Faces of Easter 1 Vol. 4	Change Colors & the Faces of Easter 1 Vol. 4	Change Colors & the Faces of Easter 1 Vol. 4
March 16	Faces of Easter 1–2 Vol. 4	Faces of Easter 1–2 Vol. 4	Faces of Easter 1–2 Vol. 4
March 23	Faces of Easter 1–3 Vol. 4	Faces of Easter 1–3 Vol. 4	Faces of Easter 1–3 Vol. 4
March 30	Faces of Easter 1–4 Vol. 4	Faces of Easter 1–4 Vol. 4	Faces of Easter 1–4 Vol. 4
April 6	Faces of Easter 1–5 Vol. 4	Faces of Easter 1–5 Vol. 4	Faces of Easter 1–7 Vol. 4
April 13 *Palm Sunday*	Faces of Easter 1–7 Vol. 4	Faces of Easter 1–7 Vol. 4	*No Class* *Children participate in* *reading of the Passion*
April 20 *Easter*	*No Class*	*No Class*	*No Class*

Appendix C

Sunday	Pre-school–K	Grades 1–3	Grades 4–8
April 27 ***Public School*** ***Vacation***	*Combined Class* Legend of the Easter Egg Vol. 4	*Combined Class* Legend of the Easter Egg Vol. 4	*Combined Class* Legend of the Easter Egg Vol. 4
May 4	The Parable of the Leaven Vol. 3	The Synagogue & the Upper Room Vol. 4	The Synagogue & the Upper Room Vol. 4
May 11	Jonah Vol. 2	The Psalms Vol. 6	The Psalms Vol. 6
May 18	Saul Changes Vol. 4	Saul Changes Vol. 4	Saul's Letters & Travels Vol. 4
May 25 ***Memorial Day w/*** ***end***	*Combined Class* Good Shepherd / World Communion Vol. 4	*Combined Class* Good Shepherd / World Communion Vol. 4	*Combined Class* Good Shepherd / World Communion Vol. 4
June 1	The Circle of the Holy Eucharist Vol. 4	The Circle of the Holy Eucharist Vol. 4	The Liturgical Synthesis Vol. 8
June 8 ***Pentecost Sunday*** Last Church School	The Mystery of Pentecost Vol. 4	The Mystery of Pentecost Vol. 4	The Church Vol. 8

GP Sample Schedule—Year 2

Sunday	Pre-school–K	Grades 1–3	Grades 4–8
Sept. 15	Circle of the Church Year Vol. 2	Circle of the Church Year Vol. 2	Circle of the Church Year Vol. 2
Sept. 22	The Holy Bible Vol. 2	The Books of the Bible Vol. 2	The Books of the Bible Vol. 2
Sept. 29	The Holy Family Vol. 2	The Falling Apart Vol. 6	Creation Vol. 2
Oct. 6	Creation Vol. 2	Abraham Vol. 6	Exodus Vol. 6
Oct. 13 *Columbus Day w/end*	The Ark & the Flood Vol. 2	Sarah Vol. 6	Moses Vol. 6
Oct. 20	The Great Family Vol. 2	Jacob	The Prophets Vol. 2
Oct. 27	The Parable of the Good Shepherd Vol. 3	The Parable of the Good Shepherd Vol. 3	The Parable of the Good Shepherd Vol. 3
Nov. 3	Baptism Vol. 3	Baptism Vol. 3	Baptism Vol. 3
Nov. 10	The Exodus Vol. 2	The Prophets Vol. 2	Isaiah Vol. 6
Nov. 17	The Ark & the Tent Vol. 2	Elijah Vol. 6	Daniel Vol. 6
Nov. 24	The Parable of the Pearl Vol. 3	The Parable of the Pearl Vol. 3	The Pearl & Mustard Seed Side by Side Vol. 3
Dec. 1 *Thanksgiving w/ end*	Combined Class Change Colors—Advent 1 Vol. 3	Combined Class Change Colors—Advent 1 Vol. 3	Combined Class Change Colors—Advent 1 Vol. 3
Dec. 8	Advent 1-2 Vol. 3	St. Nicholas Vol. 7	St. Nicholas Vol. 7
Dec. 15	*No Class* **Pageant Sunday**	*No Class* **Pageant Sunday**	*No Class* **Pageant Sunday**
Dec. 22	Advent 1-4 + peek at Xmas Vol. 3	Advent 1-4 + peek at Xmas Vol. 3	Advent 1-4 + peek at Xmas Vol. 3
Dec. 29	Combined Class The Mystery of Christmas Vol. 3	Combined Class The Mystery of Christmas Vol. 3	Combined Class The Mystery of Christmas Vol. 3
Jan. 5	Epiphany Vol. 3	Epiphany Vol. 3	Epiphany Vol. 3
Jan. 12	Intro. to Saints' Vol. 7	Expanded Intro. to Saints Vol. 7	Expanded Intro. to Saints Vol. 7

Sunday	Pre-school–K	Grades 1–3	Grades 4–8
Jan. 19 *MLK w/end*	*Combined Class* John Lewis People of Color who Inspire Series	*Combined Class* John Lewis People of Color who Inspire Series	*Combined Class* John Lewis People of Color who Inspire Series
Jan. 26	The Ark & the Temple Vol. 2	Jeremiah Vol. 6	David Vol. 6
Feb. 2	The Exile & Return Vol. 2	The Leaven Vol. 3	The Leaven & Sower Side by Side Vol. 3
Feb. 9	The Mustard Seed Vol. 3	The Mustard Seed Vol. 3	The Mustard Seed & Pearl Side by Side Vol. 3
Feb. 16 *Public School* *Vacation*	*Combined Class* The Good Samaritan Vol. 3	*Combined Class* The Good Samaritan Vol. 3	*Combined Class* The Good Samaritan Vol. 3
Feb. 23 *Public School* *Vacation*	*Combined Class* St. Valentine Vol. 7	*Combined Class* St. Valentine Vol. 7	*Combined Class* St. Valentine Vol. 7
March 2	The Pearl Vol. 3	St. Patrick Vol. 7	The Parable Games Vol. 3
March 9 *First Sunday in* *Lent*	The Mystery of Easter Vol. 4	The Mystery of Easter Vol. 4	The Greatest Parable I Vol. 8
March 16	The Greatest Parable I Vol. 8	The Greatest Parable I Vol. 8	The Greatest Parable II Vol. 8
March 23	The Greatest Parable II Vol. 8	The Greatest Parable II Vol. 8	The Greatest Parable III Vol. 8
March 30	The Greatest Parable III Vol. 8	The Greatest Parable III Vol. 8	The Greatest Parable IV Vol. 8
April 6	The Greatest Parable IV Vol. 8	The Greatest Parable IV Vol. 8	Jesus in Jerusalem Vol. 8
April 13 *Palm Sunday*	Jesus in Jerusalem Vol. 8	Jesus in Jerusalem Vol. 8	*No Class* *Children help read the* *Passion.*
April 20 *Easter* *Public School* *Vacation*	*No Class*	*No Class*	*No Class*
April 27 *Public School* *Vacation*	*Combined Class* Knowing Jesus in a New Way 1 Vol. 8	*Combined Class* Knowing Jesus in a New Way 1 Vol. 8	*Combined Class* Knowing Jesus in a New Way 1 Vol. 8
May 4	Knowing Jesus in a New Way 1-2 Vol. 8	Knowing Jesus in a New Way 1-2 Vol. 8	Knowing Jesus in a New Way 1-2 Vol. 8

Sunday	Pre-school–K	Grades 1–3	Grades 4–8
May 11	Knowing Jesus in a New Way 1-3 Vol. 8	Knowing Jesus in a New Way 1-3 Vol. 8	Knowing Jesus in a New Way 1-3 Vol. 8
May 18	Knowing Jesus in a New Way 1-4 Vol. 8	Knowing Jesus in a New Way 1-4 Vol. 8	Knowing Jesus in a New Way 1-4 Vol. 8
May 25 *Memorial Day w/ end*	*Combined Class* Knowing Jesus in a New Way 1-5 Vol. 8	*Combined Class* Knowing Jesus in a New Way 1-5 Vol. 8	*Combined Class* Knowing Jesus in a New Way 1-5 Vol. 8
June 1	Knowing Jesus in a New Way 1-6 Vol. 8	Knowing Jesus in a New Way 1-6 Vol. 8	Knowing Jesus in a New Way 1-6 Vol. 8
June 8 *Pentecost Sunday*	Knowing Jesus in a New Way 1-7 Vol. 8	Knowing Jesus in a New Way 1-7 Vol. 8	Knowing Jesus in a New Way 1-7 Vol. 8
June 15 *Trinity Sunday* **Last Church School**	The Circle of the Holy Eucharist Vol. 4	Jesus and the Twelve Vol. 4	Trinity Synthesis Vol. 2

Appendix D
Annotated List of Suggested Print Materials for Godly Play Rooms

For Your Old Testament Sacred Story Shelves

Allan, Tony. *Pharaohs and Pyramids.* Edited by Abigail Wheatley. Tulsa, OK: Usborne Publishing Ltd., 2003.

> Presents everyday life in ancient Egypt by portraying members of a wealthy family at home and away. This book can enrich the stories that reference the Pharaoh and Egypt.

Berryman, Jerome W. *The Great Family.* Large-type edition. New York: Church Publishing, 2014.

> Presents Jerome Berryman's story "The Great Family" (from *The Complete Guide to Godly Play*, Volume 2) in picture book format.

Delval, Marie-Helene. *Psalms for Young Children.* Grand Rapids, MI: Eerdmans Books for Young Readers, 2008.

> This collection of psalms, paraphrased for children, uses simple imagery to help children express their feelings using the words of the psalms. It enriches the lesson about the Psalms found in the Revised and Expanded Volume 6 of *The Complete Guide to Godly Play*.

Gallery, Philip D. *Can You Find Bible Heroes? Introducing Your Child to the Old Testament.* Cincinnati, OH: Franciscan Media, 1998.

> Children can find objects and people hidden in illustrations depicting Old Testament stories.

Hastings, Selina. *Noah's Ark: And Other Bible Stories.* New York: DK Pub, 1994.

> Stories from the books of Genesis and Exodus, together with information about life in Old Testament times.

Ladwig, Tim. *Psalm Twenty-Three.* New York: Eerdmans Books for Young Readers, 1997.

The text of the familiar psalm comparing God to a loving shepherd accompanies illustrations that show the world of love and fear faced by an urban African-American family.

Manushkin, Fran. *Miriam's Cup: A Passover Story.* 1st edition. New York: Scholastic Press, 1998.

An illustrated celebration of the role of Miriam in the Exodus story recounts how she persuaded her parents to defy the pharaoh and give birth to her brother Moses and used her miraculous well to help her people survive.

McDermott, Gerald. *Creation.* 1st edition. New York: Dutton Juvenile, 2003.

McDermott uses poetic language and abstract art to invite contemplation on God's creation.

McKellar, Shona, and Masahiro Kasuya. *Beginning of the Rainbow.* London, England: Evans Bros., 1977.

A retelling of the story of the Ark and the Flood from Genesis, chapter 9.

Mead, Joy. *The Telling Place.* Scotland, UK: Wild Goose Publications, 2002.

A book of reflections on stories of women in the Bible. Joy Mead imagines the women mentioned in the Bible as central to their own stories, rather than appearing briefly on the margins of a narrative that reflects a world perceived and led by men.

Murdoch, David. *Discoveries: Tutankhamun: The Life and Death of a Pharaoh.* New York: DK Publishing, 1998.

Relates the story of the discovery of Tutankhamun's tomb and what it revealed about the funeral rites of the pharaoh.

Petras, Ross, and Kathryn Petras. *Fandex Family Field Guides: Old Testament: Stories from the Bible.* New York: Workman Publishing Company, 2001.

Introduces important figures from the Old Testament. Each entry is illustrated with a selection of images from paintings, sculpture, and illuminations, and includes notes on names and lineage.

Poole, Susie. *A Time for Everything.* Reprint edition. Nashville, TN: B&H Kids, 2017.

An illustrated children's version of Ecclesiastes 3.

Ross, Hammer Lillian, and Kyra Teis. *Daughters of Eve: Strong Women of the Bible.* English language edition. New York: Barefoot Books, 2000.

Stories of Jewish women of the Bible who stood up for their beliefs and emerged triumphant—including Ruth, Abigail, Miriam, Zipporah, and Esther—dramatize their lives and daily struggles.

Sasso, Rabbi Sandy Eisenberg. *But God Remembered: Stories of Women from Creation to the Promised Land.* 1st edition. Woodstock, VT: Jewish Lights, 2008.

A collection of stories that gives voices and names to women from biblical and ancient times whom we seldom remember: Lillith, Serach, Bityah, and the Daughters of Z.

Seeger, Pete. *Turn! Turn! Turn!* Book and CD-ROM edition. New York: Simon & Schuster Children's Publishing, 2003.

A picture book of the well-known song by Pete Seeger, based on Ecclesiastes 3.

Swartz, Nancy Sohn. *In Our Image: God's First Creatures.* 1st edition. Woodstock, VT: Jewish Lights, 2011.

In this telling of the story of Creation, God asks all of nature to offer gifts to humankind—with the promise that the humans would care for creation in return.

Tord, Bijou Le. *Noah's Trees.* Harpercollins Children's Books, 1999.

Noah nurtures his trees, planning to give them to his sons, but God has another use for them in mind.

Tutu, Desmond, and Nancy Tillman. *Let There Be Light.* Grand Rapids, MI: Zonderkidz, 2014.

Bishop Tutu portrays the wonder and beauty of the biblical story of God's work during the seven days of creation.

Wilson, Anne. *The Lord Is My Shepherd*. Grand Rapids, MI: Eerdmans Publishing, 2003.

An illustrated version of Psalm 23.

Young, Ed. *Genesis*. First American edition. New York: Harpercollins Children's Books, 1997.

Provides the story of Creation, from the Book of Genesis.

For Your New Testament Sacred Story Shelves

Hastings, Selina. *The Birth of Jesus: And Other Bible Stories*. London: DK Publishing, 1997.

Bible stories from the early life and teachings of Jesus, including information about life in New Testament times.

Halperin, Wendy Anderson, ed. *Love Is . . .* New York: Simon & Schuster, 2005.

Love is patient. Love is kind. Love never ends . . . (from Corinthians 12). Artist Wendy Anderson Halperin brings the timeless message of love to life in watercolors.

Hastings, Selina. *Miracle of Jesus and Other Stories*. London: DK Publishing, 1996.

Bible stories about the miracles of Jesus, his Passion and Resurrection, and the deeds of Peter and Paul. All the stories are accompanied by information about life in New Testament times.

Hoffman, Mary. *Miracles: Wonders Jesus Worked*. New York: Dial, 2001.

A simple telling of nine miracles performed by Jesus with watercolor illustrations.

Hunt, Angela Elwell. *The Tale of Three Trees : A Traditional Folktale*. Abridged edition. Colorado Springs, CO: David C Cook, 2001.

The story of three little trees who dreamed of what they wanted to become when they grew up. Each of their dreams comes true in unexpected ways as they all become important parts of the story of Jesus.

Joslin, Mary, and Alison Wisenfeld. *Mary, Mother of Jesus.* First edition. Chicago: Loyola Press, 1999.

The story of Mary is told through the eyes of a wise, old woman sitting under a shady tree, with neighborhood children gathered around. It turns out that the woman is Mary herself, recounting her life with Jesus.

Wildsmith, Brian. *Jesus.* First edition. Grand Rapids, MI: Eerdmans Publishing, 2000.

Wildsmith shares the life of Jesus of Nazareth in a series of illustrations, framed by gold.

For Your Parable Shelves

Amery, Heather. *The Prodigal Son.* Tulsa, OK: Usborne Publishing Ltd., 1999.

A retelling of the Parable of the Prodigal Son with colorful illustrations.

Berryman, Jerome. *The Good Shepherd: A Picture Book for Children.* New York: Church Publishing, Inc., 2014.

This picture book is based on the Parable of the Good Shepherd (*The Complete Guide to Godly Play*, Vol. 3). It uses similar artwork to the story found in the Godly Play Room.

Carle, Eric. *The Tiny Seed.* Natick, MA: Picture Book Studio, 1987.

A creative spin on the Parable of the Sower.

dePaola, Tomie. *The Parables of Jesus.* New York: Holiday House, 1995.

This collection includes the best-known parables of Jesus: the Prodigal Son, the Mustard Seed, the Lost Sheep, and fourteen others, retold and illustrated by Tomie dePaola.

Hoffman, Mary. *Parables: Stories Jesus Told.* New York: Dial, 2000.

A collection of eight parables presented in accessible language for children and complimented with richly colored illustrations.

Scott, Bernard Brandon. *Hear Then the Parable: A Commentary on the Parables of Jesus.* Revised edition. Minneapolis: Fortress Press, 1989.

This is a resource book for Godly Play mentors and children in late childhood. It is known as an innovative literary-social reading of all the parables of Jesus.

Tord, Bijou Le. *God's Little Seeds: A Book of Parables.* Grand Rapids, MI: Eerdmans Publishing, 1998.

Focuses on the Parables of the Sower and of the Mustard Seed, demonstrating how God's little seeds can take root and grow in one's heart and life.

Reference Texts for the Bible Shelf (Also Known as the Transition Shelf)

Chandler, Fiona, and Susie McCaffrey. *Ancient World.* New York: Scholastic Inc., 2000.

Clear text, illustrations, and pictures introduce children to the history of the ancient world (10,000 BCE–500 CE).

Children's World Atlas. Revised edition. Kathleen Baker, consultant. New York: DK Children, 2011.

Facts, maps, satellite images, and local stories take the reader around the world, from Bolivia's bustling markets to carnival time in Venice.

Cross, F. L., and E. A. Livingstone, eds. *The Oxford Dictionary of the Christian Church.* 3rd revised edition. New York: Oxford University Press, 2005.

The Oxford Dictionary of the Christian Church is a one-volume reference work on all aspects of the Christian Church.

Hull, Edward. *The Wall Chart of World History: From Earliest Times to the Present.* Facsimile edition. Revised edition. New York: Barnes & Noble, 1999.

Six millennia of world history at a glance, in more than four hundred illustrations, creating a thirty-foot visual panorama of history.

McAllister, Margaret. *Women of the Bible.* New edition. Oxford: Lion Children's Books, 2013.

A collection of ten Bible stories retold from the point of view of the women involved including Noah's wife, Miriam, Ruth, Mary mother of Jesus, Pilate's wife, and Mary Magdalene.

Merriam-Webster's Student Atlas. New edition. Springfield, MA: Merriam-Webster, Inc., 2019.

A world atlas for students in grades five through eight. Includes full-color maps, photographs, and easy-to-use charts and graphs.

Nelson, Thomas. *Nelson's Student Bible Dictionary: A Complete Guide to Understanding the World of the Bible.* Edited by Ronald F. Youngblood, F. F. Bruce, and R. K. Harrison. Illustrated edition. Nashville, TN: Thomas Nelson, 2005.

Presents close to two thousand definitions, representing the best in biblical scholarship, accompanied by photographs, illustrations, charts, and maps.

Robinson, Thomas L. *Bible Timeline.* First edition. Balwyn, Australia: Thomas Nelson Inc., 1992.

An over-sized book of history during biblical times, beginning with creation through 125 CE. The pages are fold-out, for easy time-line comparison. Includes full-color illustrations.

Rose Book of Bible Charts, Maps, and Time Lines. Special edition. Torrance, CA: Rose Publishing, 2015.

Includes 216 pages of illustrations, charts, and maps on a variety of Bible topics, with two fold-outs of the genealogy of Jesus, cutaway tabernacle illustration, and Bible time line.

Bibles and Bible Stories

dePaola, Tomie. *Tomie dePaola's Book of Bible Stories.* Reprint edition. New York: Puffin Books, 2002.

This collection of stories, illustrated by Tomie dePaola, brings some of the most memorable and significant figures in the Old and New Testaments to life: Adam and Eve, Abraham and Moses, Peter, John, and Jesus.

Getty-Sullivan, Mary Ann. *God Speaks to Us in Water Stories: Bible Stories.* Collegeville, MN: Spring Arbor Distributors, 1996.

Presents Bible stories concerning water, including those about Noah and the crossing of the Red Sea.

Holy Bible: Contemporary English Version. New York: American Bible Society, 2000.

This is a good translation for children aged nine and up. We recommend having several on the Bible shelf for the children to use when asking for more detail about a story, and so on.

Maddox, Mike, and Steve Harrison. *The Graphic Bible.* 1st edition. Nashville, TN: Broadman & Holman Pub, 1998.

A book of comic-like Bible stories for preteens.

Tutu, Archbishop Desmond. *Children of God Storybook Bible.* Illustrated edition. Grand Rapids, MI: Zondervan, 2010.

Desmond Tutu retells more than fifty Bible stories in *Children of God Storybook Bible*. A Bible for children of all nationalities.

For Your Advent and Christmas Shelves

Abrams, Michelle. *Memories of the Manger.* Nashville, TN: WorthyKids, 2000.

A retelling of the story of Jesus's birth in Bethlehem from the point of view of old Mrs. Dove.

Alavedra, Joan. *They Followed A Bright Star.* New York: Putnam Juvenile, 1994.

A picture book about the shepherds and kings who were summoned to a Bethlehem stable to witness the birth of Jesus Christ.

Alary, Laura. *Look!: A Child's Guide to Advent and Christmas.* Illustrated edition. Brewster, MA: Paraclete Press, 2017.

Alary introduces children to the season of Advent—a special time for waiting and watching and paying attention to the ways God comes to us. It introduces Advent traditions such as the Jesse tree and the Advent wreath.

Amery, Heather. *The Christmas Story.* London, England: Usborne Publishing, Limited, 1990.

A retelling of the Christmas story with colorful illustrations.

Blumen, John. *The Friendly Beasts.* Minneapolis: Augsburg Fortress Pub, 1997.

An old English Christmas carol in which the friendly stable beasts tell of the gifts they have given to the newborn Child.

Byrd, Robert. *Saint Francis and the Christmas Donkey.* 1st edition. New York: Dutton Juvenile, 2000.

Saint Francis stumbles upon a sad donkey and tells him about the wonderful history the donkey has in the Christian religion as the animal who carried Mary to Nazareth when she was pregnant with Baby Jesus.

dePaola, Tomie. *Mary: The Mother of Jesus.* 1st edition. New York: Holiday House, 1995.

DePaola uses scripture and church tradition to narrate the story of Mary's life alongside original artwork.

Dunbar, Joyce. *This Is the Star.* 1st U.S. edition. San Diego: Harcourt Childrens Books, 1996.

A retelling of the Christmas story with a focus on the star that led the Magi to the Christ child.

Ganeri, Anita. *The Story of Christmas.* 1st U.S. edition. Boston: DK Children, 1995.

A retelling of the Christmas story, illustrated with photographs of young children reenacting the parts of Mary, Joseph, the angels, the Wise Men, and the local villagers.

Hawthorne, Lara. *Silent Night.* Illustrated edition. London: Frances Lincoln Children's Books, 2018.

The beloved hymn "Silent Night" is brought to life with beautiful illustrations.

Jeffers, Susan. *Silent Night.* Gift edition. New York: Dutton Juvenile, 2003.

A visual interpretation of the beloved Christmas carol.

L'Engle, Madeleine, and A. Richard Turner. *The Glorious Impossible.* New York: Simon & Schuster Children's Publishing, 1990.

L'Engle's narrative of Jesus's annunciation, birth, childhood, ministry, death, and resurrection are accompanied by Giotto's frescoes from the Scrovegni Chapel in Padua. Could also be placed on the Lent/Easter shelves.

Matuszak, Pat, and Rick Osborne. *Legend of the Christmas Tree Board Book.* Grand Rapids, MI: Zonderkidz, 2002.

This picture book explains how the evergreen tree first became a symbol of Christmas and a way to tell people about God.

Osborne, Rick, and James Griffin. *Legend of the Christmas Stocking.* Grand Rapids, MI: Zonderkidz, 2004.

This book explores the origins of the Christmas stocking, inspired by the life of Saint Nicolas.

Robbins, Ruth. *Baboushka and the Three Kings.* New York: HMH Books for Young Readers, 1960.

The Russian folktale about an old woman's endless search for the Christ Child.

Slate, Joseph. *Who Is Coming to Our House?* Board book edition. New York: G.P. Putnam's Sons Books for Young Readers, 2001.

A modern Christmas classic about how the animals prepare a cozy welcome for the baby Jesus.

The National Gallery. *The First Christmas.* London: Frances Lincoln Children's Books, 2010.

This book tells the classical "Christmas" story beginning with the Annunciation and ending with the Holy Family fleeing to Egypt. The illustrations are paintings from the National Gallery in London.

Weber, Susan. *Nativities of the World.* Kaysville, UT: Gibbs Smith, 2013.

Nearly one hundred nativities from all over the world are collected here. Artisans from locales as diverse as the Czech Republic, Guyana, Burkina Faso, and Bangladesh are represented.

Westerlund, Kate. *The Message of the Birds.* Hong Kong: Minedition Michael Neugebauer Publishing Ltd., 2013.

A timeless message of how peace can spread from one person to another, ideal for Christmas time, and throughout the year.

Wijngaard, Juan, ed. *The Nativity.* 1st edition. New York: Lothrop Lee & Shepard, 1990.

A retelling of the birth of Christ, with illustrations.

Wojciechowski, Susan. *The Christmas Miracle of Jonathan Toomey.* Anniversary edition. Cambridge, MA: Candlewick, 2015.

Toomey is the best woodcarver in the valley. He lives alone and never smiles. One winter's day, a widow and her young son approach him with a gentle request that leads to a joyful miracle.

For Your Lent and Easter Shelves

Alary, Laura. *Make Room: A Child's Guide to Lent and Easter.* Illustrated edition. Brewster, MA: Paraclete Press, 2016.

Alary introduces children to the season Lent (a time to prepare for Easter) and the traditions of Easter.

Amery, Heather, and N. Young. *The Usborne Easter Story*. London: Usborne, 2006.

A colorful retelling of the story of Easter.

Carlson, Melody. *Benjamin's Box: The Story of the Resurrection Eggs*. Revised edition. Grand Rapids, MI: Zonderkidz, 2008.

The reader learns about Jesus along with Benjamin as he follows Jesus through Jerusalem to find out who this man really is.

Heyer, Carol. *The Easter Story*. Nashville, TN: Ideals Children's Books, 1990.

Artist Carol Heyer illustrates this beautiful retelling of the Easter story.

Maier, Paul L. *The Very First Easter*. Illustrated edition. Saint Louis, MO: Concordia Publishing, 2004.

Christopher, a ten-year old boy, asks to hear the real story of Easter. His family sits him down and reads him the story of Easter straight from the Gospel of Luke.

Perchyshyn, Natalie. *A Kid's Guide to Decorating Ukrainian Easter Eggs*. 1st edition. Minneapolis, MN: Ukrainian Gift Shop, 2000.

Contains systematic instruction designed to give the basic skills needed for decorating pysanky.

Steig, William. *Sylvester and the Magic Pebble*. New York: Simon & Schuster Books for Young Readers, 2004.

This classic children's book is a story of life, death, and resurrection. Sylvester the donkey finds a magic pebble that fulfills his wishes until everything goes horribly wrong and he becomes a rock. It takes an act of love and hope to bring him back to life. A story of resurrection to enrich your Lent/Easter shelf.

Strong, Dina. *Hosanna and Alleluia: Stories of Holy Week and Easter*. New York: Morehouse Publishing, 1997.

A large (11-by-17-inch) format book, good for sharing the story of Holy Week and Easter with large groups.

For Your Pentecost Shelves

Alary, Laura. *Breathe: A Child's Guide to Ascension, Pentecost, and the Growing Time.* Brewster, MA: Paraclete Press, 2021.

This book explores the comings and goings of Jesus and the Spirit through retellings of the biblical stories of Ascension and Pentecost, interwoven with contemporary reflections from the point of view of a child.

Hutto, Rebekah McLeod. *The Day When God Made Church: A Child's First Book About Pentecost.* Brewster, MA: Paraclete Press, 2016.

This book helps children understand and celebrate the birthday of the Church.

For Your Saint / Hero Shelves

Asim, Jabari. *Preaching to the Chickens: The Story of Young John Lewis.* Illustrated edition. New York: Nancy Paulsen Books, 2016.

A story about the boyhood of civil rights leader John Lewis. John wants to be a preacher when he grows up—but why wait? When John is put in charge of the family farm's flock of chickens, he begins preaching to the chickens!

dePaola, Tomie. *The Lady of Guadalupe.* New York: Holiday House, 1980.

The story of the patron saint of Mexico, the Lady of Guadalupe, told and illustrated by Tomie dePaola.

Haskins, Jim, and Kathleen Benson. *John Lewis in the Lead.* Reprint edition. New York: Lee & Low Books, 2011.

A biography of John Lewis, one of the Big Six civil rights leaders of the 1960s.

Kimmel, Eric A. *Brother Wolf, Sister Sparrow.* 1st edition. New York: Holiday House, 2003.

From Saint Francis to Saint Brigid, this book is about the relationships between the beasts of the field and the birds of the sky and twelve holy men and women who cared for them.

Milligan, Bryce. *Brigid's Cloak.* Illustrated edition. Grand Rapids, MI: Eerdmans Books for Young Readers, 2005.

This story retells an ancient tale about one of Ireland's most beloved saints. On the day she is born Brigid receives a brilliant blue cloak from a mysterious Druid. It leads her to the Christ Child.

Near, Holly. *The Great Peace March.* New York: Henry Holt and Co., 1997.

A song inspired by an actual peace march, this work celebrates peace and the courage to make it real.

Norris, Kathleen. *The Holy Twins: Benedict and Scholastica.* New York: Puffin, 2011.

Norris explores how the childhoods and lives of twins Benedict and Scholastica and how their relationship helped Benedict with monastic reform.

Pochocki, Ethel. *The Blessing of Beasts.* Brewster, MA: Paraclete Press, 2007.

Francesca the skunk and other creatures learn about valuing and caring for all of God's creation, even those who smell.

Scott, Lesbia. *I Sing a Song of the Saints of God.* Harrisburg, PA: Morehouse Publishing, 1991.

This presentation of the classic hymn draws children into the world of saints and their life adventures.

Stoeckl, Jay. *Saint Francis and Brother Duck.* Brewster, MA: Paraclete Press, 2013.

The life of Saint Francis comes to life in this graphic novel based on the real-life events of the saint's life, set in the mountains of Italy.

Weatherford, Carole Boston. *Moses: When Harriet Tubman Led Her People to Freedom.* 1st edition. New York: Hyperion Book CH, 2006.

A tribute to Harriet Tubman, the woman who earned the name Moses for her heroic role in the Underground Railroad.

Resources to Place under the Story of the Church

(*The Complete Guide to Godly Play*, Volume 8, Lesson 14)

Bunting, Eve. *Night of the Gargoyles.* Reprint edition. New York: Clarion Books, 1999.

    A story of what happens at night when the gargoyles come to life.

Ciagà, Graziella Leyla. *Cathedrals of the World.* Revised edition. Vercelli, Italy: White Star Publishers, 2012.

    This book takes the reader on a journey through Christianity by way of its most well-known architectural creations such as St. Mark's Basilica, Westminster Cathedral, Johnson's Crystal Cathedral in Garden Grove, California, and Richard Meier's Jubilee Church in Rome.

Field, John. *Kingdom Power and Glory: A Historical Guide to Westminster Abbey.* 4th edition. London: Third Millennium Pub. Ltd., 2009.

    An illustrated historical guide to Westminster Abbey.

Halliday, Sonia, Laura Lushington, and Tim Dowley. *The Bible in Stained Glass.* Ridgefield, CT: Bible Society, 1990.

    Full-color reproductions, with full descriptions of the windows and their iconography, of some of the most spectacular and historic stained-glass windows of Europe.

Macaulay, David. *Cathedral: The Story of Its Construction.* Boston, MA: Sandpiper, 1981.

    This book takes the reader on a journey to visit the fictional people of twelfth-, thirteenth-, and fourteenth-century Europe, whose dreams, like Cathedral, stand the test of time.

Washington National Cathedral Guidebook. 2016. https://shop.cathedral.org /washington-national-cathedral-guidebook.html.

    This takes the reader on a tour of the Washington National Cathedral.

Prayer and Worship

(These can be placed in a basket near the liturgical furniture or in a meditation/prayer corner.)

Boling, Ruth L. *Come Worship with Me: A Journey through the Church Year.* Illustrated edition. Louisville, KY: Westminster John Knox Press, 2010.

An illustrated children's book about Advent, Christmas, Palm Sunday, and Easter through the eyes of a church mouse.

Cotner, June, ed. *Amazing Graces: Prayers and Poems for Children.* New York: HarperCollins Children's Books, 2001.

A collection of verses by Robert Browning, Ralph Waldo Emerson, Madeleine L'Engle and Nikki Grimes, and other young poets.

Dearborn, Sabrina. *A Child's Book of Blessings.* Concord, MA: Barefoot Books, 1999.

Blessings for everyday events from dawn until dusk, for special activities and for specific times of the year.

Jelenek, Frank. *Journey to the Heart: Centering Prayer for Children.* Brewster, MA: Paraclete Press, 2007.

Frank Jelenek shows young children how to do centering prayer.

Kidd, Pennie. *Teach Me to Pray.* Illustrated edition. Chicago: Loyola Press, 1999.

This book uses a story to help young children learn how to pray. In the story, a boy, a girl, their parents, their grandparents, and the nice lady next door all want to pray, but nothing seems to work. On their mission to learn how to pray, they discover the "secret" to talking with God.

MacBeth, Sybil. *Praying in Color Kid's Edition.* Brewster, MA: Paraclete Press, 2009.

This book introduces children to MacBeth's practice of "praying in color." Using the simple act of doodling, children are led to pray for all sorts of things with just some paper and colored pencils.

Moore, Anna V. Ostenso. *Today Is a Baptism Day.* Illustrated edition. New York: Church Publishing, 2018.

> An introduction to baptism for children and families of many Christian traditions.

Simpson, Clare. *Why Do We Have to Be So Quiet in Church? And 12 Other Questions Kids Have.* Brewster, MA: Paraclete Press, 2012.

> This book explores questions young children naturally have about church: Why do we have to be so quiet in church? Does God hear me when I sing? Why do we say "Amen" at the end of everything?

Thomas, Adam. *The Lord's Prayer: Learning the Words Jesus Taught.* CreateSpace Independent Publishing Platform, 2017.

> The Lord's Prayer through words and photography, to help young children learn the words for the first time and their parents to learn them anew.

Walter, Wangerin. *Water Come Down.* Minneapolis: Augsburg Books, 1999.

> This story introduces children to the meaning of baptism.

Berryman, Jerome W. *Silence.* New York: Church Publishing, 2020.

> This illustrated book for children captures the mindfulness, measured pace, and pauses that children experience in the Godly Play circle.

Lemniscates, Carme. *Silence.* 1st edition. Washington, DC: Magination Press, 2012.

> Silence encourages children to stop, listen, and reflect on their experiences and the world around them.

Buscaglia, Leo. *The Fall of Freddie the Leaf: A Story of Life for All Ages.* Thorofare, NJ: Slack Incorporated, 1982.

> This story follows Freddie and his companions as their leaves change with the passing seasons and the coming of winter, finally falling to the ground with winter's snow. It is a resource for all those experiencing grief and loss.

Chard, Sylvia, and Yvonne Kogan. *From My Side: Being a Child.* Lewisville, NC: Gryphon House, 2009.

This beautiful book, filled with hundreds of color photographs from many different countries, invites us to look through a window into the lives of children everywhere.

Emerson, Ralph Waldo. *Father, We Thank You.* 1st edition. New York: SeaStar Books, 2000.

An illustrated poem celebrating the joys of creation.

Hutchison, Roger. *My Favorite Color Is Blue. Sometimes.: A Journey Through Loss with Art and Color.* Brewster, MA: Paraclete Press, 2017.

A picture book to guide the reader through different emotions and reactions related to grieving.

Kunkel, Jeff. *What Scares Me and What I Do About It: Stories and Pictures by Sunday School Kids.* Minneapolis, MN: Augsburg Fortress Pub., 2003.

In text and pictures, children describe what makes them afraid and how they deal with their fear.

Kushner, Rabbi Lawrence, and Karen Kushner. *What Does God Look Like?* Woodstock, VT: SkyLight Paths, 2001.

A simple way for young children to explore the ways we "see" God.

Kushner, Rabbi Lawrence, and Karen Kushner. *Where Is God?* Woodstock, VT: SkyLight Paths, 2000.

A book about finding God in the everyday things of life.

Main, Judith Lang. *A Is for Altar, B Is for Bible.* Chicago, IL: Catechesis of Good Shepherd Publications, 2007.

Using the familiar foundation of the ABCs, *A Is for Altar, B Is for Bible* presents some of the essential elements of our Christian faith.

Saint-Exupéry, Antoine de, and Richard Howard. *The Little Prince.* 1st edition. San Diego: Harcourt, 2000.

An aviator whose plane is forced down in the Sahara Desert encounters a little prince from a small planet who relates his adventures in seeking the secret of what is important in life.

Sasso, Rabbi Sandy Eisenberg. *I Am God's Paintbrush.* 1st edition. Woodstock, VT: SkyLight Paths, 2009.

This invites children of all faiths and backgrounds to encounter God through everyday experience and the imagination.

Scholes, Katharine, and Sierra Club Books. *Peace Begins With You.* Reissue edition. New York: Little, Brown Books for Young Readers, 1994.

Explains, in simple terms, the concept of peace, why conflicts occur, how they can be resolved in positive ways, and how to protect peace.

Tutu, Archbishop Desmond, and Douglas Carlton Abrams. *God's Dream.* Illustrated edition. Somerville, MA: Candlewick, 2010.

Archbishop Tutu distills his philosophy of unity and forgiveness for the very young.

Wood, Douglas. *Old Turtle and the Broken Truth.* 1st edition. New York: Scholastic Press, 2003.

People of all ages have been inspired by the stirring message of Old Turtle, the award-winning wisdom tale of peace. Now Old Turtle returns in a story about love, acceptance, and the nature of truth.

Barth, Edna. *Witches, Pumpkins, and Grinning Ghosts: The Story of the Halloween Symbols.* Annotated edition. New York: Clarion Books, 2000.

Edna Barth explores the multicultural origins and evolution of the familiar and not-so-familiar symbols and legends of Halloween.

Penner, Lucille Recht. *Celebration: The Story of American Holidays.* 1st edition. New York: Simon & Schuster, 1993.

Penner examines the history of thirteen American holidays, including Halloween, Memorial Day, and the birthday of Martin Luther King Jr.

Appendix E
Chart of Six Conditions That Nurture Relational Consciousness in Children

Space, Process, Imagination, Relationship, Intimacy, Trust

	Conceptual Level	Operational Level	How the Godly Play method delivers the conditions
1. Space	*Physical space:* Positively or negatively influences spiritual well-being (Nye, 2009). The way a space looks and feels communicates the relative value given to the activity that will take place in the space (Nye, 2009). The choice of materials used or provided communicates the relative value of the work being done in the space (Nye, 2009).	*Physical space:* Space used for spiritual nurture should be prepared with an eye to beauty and order, similar to the same care given to the space used for worship by adults (Nye, 2009). The space and the materials used should be carefully maintained, e.g. clean rugs, dusted shelves, high quality materials, beautiful materials (Nye, 2009).	*Physical space:* The Godly Play Method for a carefully prepared environment (Berryman, 1991, 2009). Low shelves used to carefully display materials, giving children of all ages easy access to everything (Berryman, 1991, 2009). Beautifully crafted materials used for presenting lessons (stories from the Bible, and lessons about the way the community worships), and high quality art materials are provided for the children to use as they reflect on the lessons or other important things happening in their lives (Berryman, 1991). Mentor models how to care for the materials, e.g. showing how to remove the material from its container, how to return the material to its container so that the next person will have everything needed (Berryman, 2009). Mentor encourages the children to care for the space themselves, e.g. providing them with the tools to clean up spills, water plants, dust shelves, and more (Berryman, 2009).

	Conceptual Level	Operational Level	How the Godly Play method delivers the conditions
Space continued	*Emotional space:* The freedom to be yourself (Nye, 2009). Safe space for the child to share different ideas and feelings without fear of judgment (Nye, 2009). Safe space for the child to think and speak about serious and/or important things (Nye, 2009). Respect for the child's private thoughts (Nye, 2009).	*Emotional space:* Teachers can provide this by working to honor and respect all of the ideas the children offer regarding the serious and the mundane. Teachers can make descriptive comments about a child's work (artwork, written work) as opposed to a judgment-laden comment, e.g. "That's good!" Or "That's beautiful." Even though these comments are positive, they carry with them the possibility that sometimes the child does or says something that is somehow bad or wrong. Teachers should take care not to force participation in a conversation or activity, to give the child space for private thoughts or time for reflection.	*Emotional space:* Mentors provide emotional space by learning to facilitate spiritual conversations using a model called "wondering," e.g. mentors ask, "I wonder what the most important part of the story is?" And "I wonder what this could really be or where it really is?" As the children offer their thoughts the mentor encourages everyone saying, "Hmm . . . that could be. I wonder?" In this way all ideas are encouraged and respected and over time the children can feel safe offering their ideas, without fear of judgment by the mentor (Berryman, 2009). Children learn to respect one another's ideas and thoughts by watching the mentor model this behavior. If, for example, a child in the circle tells another child their idea is silly or "wrong", mentors are taught to say something like, "Sometimes new ideas sound silly or strange, don't they?" In this way both children feel respected for their thoughts and no one is judged as being wrong or bad for their ideas (Berryman, 2009). No one is forced to answer the wondering questions, thus respecting some of the children's needs to keep their thoughts private, or to wait until they feel safer or more comfortable sharing with both the mentors and their peers. This same respect is given to the children during response time. The mentors learn not to comment on a child's work unless invited, and then to take care to make descriptive comments as opposed to judgment-laden comments, e.g. saying something like, "This picture is very dark" or "Tell me what's happening in your picture," instead of saying, "I love your picture," or "It's beautiful."

	Conceptual Level	Operational Level	How the Godly Play method delivers the conditions
Space continued	*Auditory space:* Auditory space is about allowing for silence or times of quiet to make space for the children to think or reflect. When the process of thinking is interrupted too quickly with another question, the children are discouraged from engaging deeply (Nye, 2009).	*Auditory space.* Leave intentional periods of silence after asking an open-ended question. Nye (2009) suggests counting to seven internally as a way of practicing this.	*Auditory space:* Silence is an intentional part of the method. This can be seen in all aspects of a session. The Story / Lesson: During many of the story or lesson presentations the mentor is quietly moving material, not filling up the space with words. For example, when the people are traveling through the desert (a large container of sand in the classroom) on their journey, it is so quiet that you can hear the wooden figures as they "crunch" against the sand. The Wondering: During the wondering time, mentors ask open-ended questions. They are taught to allow for silence between questions so the children can think about the question internally, and sometimes share what they are thinking with their teacher and peers (Berryman, 2009). Response time: During response time the children are free to talk to one another or the teachers in the room. However, the mentors monitor the noise level carefully to see if it is disrupting or distracting anyone as they work with a story or art material (Berryman, 2009). Mentors do not interrupt work, either that being done by individuals or small groups, unless it is disrupting others in the room (Berryman, 2009).

	Conceptual Level	Operational Level	How the Godly Play method delivers the conditions
2. Process	In order for relational consciousness to flourish, there must be a focus on process as opposed to product (Nye, 2009). "Production suggests that the end result is all important, and that this kind of work can be 'finished,' freeing us up to do something else. But spiritual life is an ongoing piece of work, not something to be completed or get prizes for" (Nye, 2009, p. 46).	Limiting focus on completed artwork, performances of any kind, or the typical "show and tell" activity often associated with education (Nye, 2009).	Focuses on process, as opposed to product, by giving children significant time to work on their own with the materials in the room, to create artwork for themselves instead of a particular project that will be sent home or displayed in some way (Berryman, 2009). Mentors comment on a child's work only when invited, and then only to make descriptive as opposed to judgment-laden comments (Berryman, 2009).
3. Imagination	In order for relational consciousness to flourish, children need to be encouraged to use their imaginative faculties (Nye, 2009). This is not about presenting lessons in an imaginative or creative way, but about encouraging the child's use of his or her own imagination as they wonder and think about their spiritual lives. "Spirituality depends on our being open and willing to go deeper. Imagination and creativity can resource this, but often very clear permission has to be given this is 'okay'" (Nye, 2009, p. 49).	"Include imaginative 'warm up' exercises, e.g. 'How many different things could this prop be?!'" (Nye, 2009 p. 50). "Resist the urge to steer away from the apparently crazy comments or suggestions that children are bound to make sometimes. Pay serious attention to the off-the-wall suggestions . . ." (Nye, 2009, p. 50). "Give opportunities for children to choose for themselves what to paint, draw, or make in response to the input" (Nye, 2009, p. 50).	Encourages children to use their imaginations, particularly in the process of "wondering" described above. Mentors are trained, for example, to accept all of the answers offered by the children during the time of wondering without judgment (Berryman, 2009a). Example: Mentors will not even say, "Yes, that's good." This seems affirming, but it could shut down the imaginations of the other children in the circle if they think their own thoughts might not be considered "good." Instead, as each idea is offered the mentor will nod and say something like, "That could be. I wonder?" This invites the other children in the room to offer their own thoughts without fear of being wrong. Children work with the lesson material, sometimes simply re-telling the story or using their imaginations to add things so as to draw connections to something that might be happening in their own lives (Berryman, 2009).

	Conceptual Level	Operational Level	How the Godly Play method delivers the conditions
4. Relationship	Relational consciousness is deeply rooted in the child's experience of relationships so it follows that attending to relationships must be an explicit part of its nurture.	Nye (2009) proposes that this is done by modeling and supporting an atmosphere of respect and openness for the ideas and needs of everyone in the space. This supports the notion that each person's spiritual perspective is valuable and helps everyone relate more openly with one another, without fear of judgment (Nye, 2009).	Relationships are carefully attended to including the child's relationships with God, with their peers, with the teachers, with their parents and siblings, with the members of their religious community (Berryman, 2009). Mentors are taught to model a listening, respectful atmosphere by carefully valuing all that is offered by the children in the room and to encourage that same respect among the children (Berryman, 2009). Practical examples: Children are encouraged to sit in the circle without touching or bothering the person beside them, to walk around a person's work when it is laid on the floor rather than stepping on it, to ask if it is okay to share materials and to honor the fact that sometimes a person may need to work alone on something and will therefore say "no" to a request to share (Berryman, 2009). Mentors also work to "level" the relationship between themselves and the children. They sit on the floor or in low chairs so that they do not stand above the children physically, and do not pose as "experts" on God in the room but instead as fellow wonderers (Berryman, 2009). Children are encouraged to respect one another's choices and carefully supported as they work out disputes amongst themselves (Berryman, 2009). Substantial time is given for children to deepen their relationship with God, making time for quiet reflection, providing them with multiple tools for reflection including art supplies, books, and the artifacts used to present the stories from the Bible (Berryman, 2009).

	Conceptual Level	Operational Level	How the Godly Play method delivers the conditions
5. Intimacy	Conversing about deeply personally held convictions, ideas, questions, feelings, requires a sense of trust and closeness (Nye, 2009). There are many things that thwart the development of intimacy, including fear of being judged on how much one knows, that the ideas one has are not the "right" ideas, or that someone might laugh at what is said or think it is silly (Nye, 2009).	Building trust that everything offered in the space will be respected and taken seriously is achieved by modeling and practicing respect and seriousness for what the children say authentically and consistently over a long period of time (Nye, 2009).	Does not rush children to share their innermost thoughts and feelings, working instead to build trust and provide the time needed for intimacy to develop (Berryman, 2009). All ideas are met with respect by the teacher and the Mentor works to help the other children in the room to be respectful of their peers (Berryman, 2009). Questions are asked, opportunities to make choices are given, but the children are given the freedom to speak or not to speak, to sit quietly or work with the materials provided. Given time, the children will often verbalize some of their deeply personal thoughts and feelings, but this is not a goal (Berryman, 2009). The goal is to give them the tools and the space necessary to do this interior work both in the room, and long after they leave the room (Berryman, 2009).

	Conceptual Level	Operational Level	How the Godly Play method delivers the conditions
6. Trust	Trust is defined here as less about the kind of trust needed for intimacy discussed above, and more about the trust the adult leader has for the children and for spirituality in general. For relational consciousness to flourish in children, they must trust themselves and this often begins with the support of an adult; with the adult communicating trust in the child (Nye, 2009). If children are going to trust their own spiritual experiences, they need models that similarly trust themselves. If, for example, children do not hear adults talking about, wondering about, sharing their own spiritual lives openly, it will not feel safe for them to do the same so they discard it (Nye, 2009).	Trust is evident, or absent, in the view adults take of themselves when working with children. If the adult is controlling or authoritative trust is undermined. For example if the adult says, "The important point of this story is . . ." it suggests a lack of trust in God to communicate what is most important and a lack of trust in the child to hear what is most important for him or her on that day. If the adult authoritatively says, "Easter is a happy time," it implies a lack of trust in the child's feelings about Easter (Nye, 2009).	Mentors model a comfort in exploring the deep meaning of the stories shared, and an attitude of imagination and wonder regarding the questions of meaning and purpose in life (Berryman, 2009). Mentors are careful not to direct the children as they make choices about their work, communicating trust in the child to make the choices that are best given their specific needs (Berryman, 2009). Mentors support children as they work out disputes, sharing materials, etc., communicating trust in the abilities of the children to work their way through difficult situations not just in the room, but beyond (Berryman, 2009).

Appendix F

Young Person's Drawing of a Cross

41

Bibliography

Allen, Holly Catterton (2021). *Forming Resilient Children: The Role of Spiritual Formation for Healthy Development.* Downers Grove, IL: InterVarsity Press.

Anthony, M. J. (Ed.) (2006). *Perspectives on Children's Spiritual Formation: Four Views.* Nashville, TN: Broadman & Holman Publishers.

Aten, J. D., Moore, M., Denney, R. M., Bayne, T., Stagg, A., Owens, S., . . . Jones, C. (2008). God images following Hurricane Katrina in South Mississippi: An exploratory study. *Journal of Psychology and Theology*, 36(4), 249–257. doi: 10.1177/009164710803600401.

Berge, J. M., Hoppmann, C., Hanson, C., Neumark-Sztainer, D. (2013). Perspectives about family meals from single-headed and dual-headed households: A qualitative analysis. *Journal of the Academy of Nutrition and Dietetics*, 113, 1632–1639. doi:10.1016/j.jand.2013.08.023.

Berryman, Jerome (1991). *Godly Play: An Imaginative Approach to Religious Education.* Minneapolis, MN: Augsburg Press.

Berryman, Jerome (2008). Cheryl Minor, consulting editor. *The Complete Guide to Godly Play,* Volume 7. Revised and expanded. New York: Church Publishing, Inc.

Berryman, Jerome (2009). Cheryl Minor, consulting editor. *Teaching Godly Play: How to Mentor the Spiritual Development of Children.* Revised and expanded. New York: Church Publishing, Inc.

Berryman, Jerome (2012). Cheryl Minor, consulting editor. *The Complete Guide to Godly Play,* Volume 8. Revised and expanded. New York: Church Publishing, Inc.

Berryman, Jerome (2013). *The Spiritual Guidance of Children: Montessori, Godly Play and the Future.* New York: Church Publishing, Inc.

Berryman, Jerome (2017). Rosemary Beales and Cheryl Minor, consulting editors. *The Complete Guide to Godly Play,* Volume 2. Revised and expanded. New York: Church Publishing, Inc.

Berryman, Jerome (2017). Rosemary Beales and Cheryl Minor, consulting editors. *The Complete Guide to Godly Play*, Volume 3. Revised and expanded. New York: Church Publishing, Inc.

Berryman, Jerome (2018). *Stories of God at Home: A Godly Play Approach.* New York: Church Publishing, Inc.

Berryman, Jerome (2018). Rosemary Beales and Cheryl Minor, consulting editors. *The Complete Guide to Godly Play*, Volume 4. Revised and expanded. New York: Church Publishing, Inc.

Berryman, Jerome (2021). Rosemary Beales and Cheryl Minor, consulting editors. *The Complete Guide to Godly Play*, Volume 6. Revised and expanded. New York: Church Publishing, Inc.

Bowen Family Therapy, http://www.psychpage.com/learning/library/counseling /bowen.html, accessed 03-14-19.

Bruner, Jerome (1960). *The Process of Education.* Cambridge, MA: Harvard University Press.

Campbell, J. D., Yoon, D. P., and Johnstone, B. (2010). Determining relationships between physical health and spiritual experience, religious practices, and con-gregational support in a heterogeneous medical sample. *Journal of Religion and Health*, 49(1), 3–17. doi:10.1007/s10943-008-9227-5.

Edens, K. M., & Potter, E. F. (2001). Promoting conceptual understanding through pictorial representation. *Studies in Art Education* 42(3), 214–233.

Eisenberg, M. E., Olson, R. E., Neumark-Sztainer, D., Story, M., Bearinger, L. H. Correlations between family meals and psychosocial well-being among adoles-cents. *The Archives of Pediatric and Adolescent Medicine.* 2004;158(8):792–796. doi: 10.1001/archpedi.158.8.792.

Fairless, Caroline (2000). *Children at Worship: Congregations in Bloom.* New York: Church Publishing, Inc.

Fisher, John (2004). Feeling good, living life: A spiritual health measure for young children. *Journal of Beliefs and Values*, 25(3), 307–315. doi: 10.1080/1361767042000306121.

Fowler, James (1981). *Stages of Faith: The Psychology of Human Development.* New York: Harper & Row.

Gavazzi S. M., S. A. Anderson, and R. M Sabatelli. "Family Differentiation, Peer Differentiation, and Adolescent Adjustment in a Clinical Sample." *Journal of Adolescent Research* 8, no. 2 (1993): 205–225. doi:10.1177/074355489382005

Glick, R. L., Berlin, J. S., Fishkind, A. B., & Zeller, S. (2008). *Emergency Psychiatry: Principles and Practice.* Philadelphia: Lippincott, Williams, & Wilkins.

Graham, S., Furr, S., Flowers, C., and Burke, M. (2001). Religion and spirituality in coping with stress. *Counseling and Values,* 46(1), 2–13. Retrieved from http://www.highbeam.com/doc/1G1-79370592.html.

Hay, David, and Nye, Rebecca (2006). *The Spirit of the Child.* Revised edition. London: Jessica Kingsley Publishers. Original work published 1998.

Houg, B.L. (2008). The role of spirituality in the ongoing recovery process of female sexual abuse survivors. Doctoral dissertation, University of Minnesota. Retrieved from *ProQuest Dissertations and Theses* (document ID: 304512145).

Hyde, Brendan (2008). Weaving the threads of meaning: A characteristic of children's spirituality and its implications for religious education. *British Journal of Religious Education,* 30(3), 235–245. doi: 10.1080/01416200802170169.

Lopez, Barry (1990). *Crow and Weasel.* San Francisco, CA: Northpoint Press.

McClain, Rebecca (2017). *Graceful Nurture: Using Godly Play with Adults.* New York: Church Publishing, Inc.

Meisenhelder, J. B., and Marcum, J. P. (2009). Terrorism, post-traumatic stress, coping strategies, and spiritual outcomes. *Journal of Religion and Health,* 48(1), 46–57. doi:10.1007/s10943-008-9192-z.

Montessori, Maria (1970). *The Child in the Family.* New York: Discus/Avon.

Montessori, Maria (1982). *The Secret Life of Childhood.* New York: Ballantine Books.

Nichols, L. M., and Hunt, B. (2011). The significance of spirituality for individuals with chronic illness: Implications for mental health counseling. *Journal of Mental Health Counseling,* 33(1), 51–66. Retrieved from http://amhca.metapress.com/link.asp?id=0255441189523j738.

Nye, Rebecca (2009). *Children's Spirituality: What It Is and Why It Matters.* London: Church House Publishing.

Smith, C. and Denton, M. (2005). *Soul Searching: The Religious and Spiritual Life of American Teenagers.* New York: Oxford University Press.

Smith, J. L. (2009). Spiritual coping in children diagnosed with cancer. Doctoral dissertation, George Fox University. Retrieved from *ProQuest Dissertations and Theses* (document ID: 855629644).

Smith, J. Z. (1987). *To Take Place: Toward Theory in Ritual.* Chicago: University of Chicago Press.

Stonehouse, C., and May, S. (2010). *Listening to Children on the Spiritual Journey: Guidance for Those Who Teach and Nurture.* Grand Rapids, MI: Baker Academic.

Westerhoff, John (2012). *Will Our Children Have Faith?* Revised and expanded. New York: Morehouse Publishing. Original work published 1976.

Wink, P., Dillon, M., and Larsen, B. (2005). Religion as moderator of the depression-health connection: Findings from a longitudinal study. *Research on Aging* 27, 197–220. doi: 10.1177/0164027504270483.

Wuthnow, Robert (1999). *Growing Up Religious.* Boston: Beacon Press.

Pickhardt, Carl (2013). *Surviving Your Child's Adolescence: How to Understand, and Even Enjoy, the Rocky Road to Independence.* Hoboken, NJ: Jossey-Bass.

Zanowski, S. C. (2009). Spiritual coping, distress, and symptoms of posttraumatic stress disorder following traumatic injury. Doctoral dissertation, Marquette University. Retrieved from *ProQuest Dissertations and Theses* (document ID: 304919311).

CPSIA information can be obtained
at www.ICGtesting.com
Printed in the USA
JSHW022011150522
25828JS00005B/7